JEREMIAH
AND THE NEW COVENANT

JEREMIAH
AND THE NEW COVENANT

BY

W. F. LOFTHOUSE, D.D.

AUTHOR OF
"ETHICS AND ATONEMENT"
"ALTAR, CROSS, AND COMMUNITY," ETC.

LONDON
STUDENT CHRISTIAN MOVEMENT
32 RUSSELL SQUARE, W.C.1
1925

First Published November 1925

*Made and Printed in Great Britain
by Turnbull & Spears, Edinburgh*

CONTENTS

CHAPTER   PAGE

CHRONOLOGICAL TABLE vii

I. "NOT FOR AN AGE BUT FOR ALL TIME" . 1

II. THE YOUTH AND HIS CALL . . . 14

III. "THE TIMES ARE OUT OF JOINT" . . 40

IV. A GREAT RELIGIOUS MOVEMENT . . . 62

V. REACTION 88

VI. THE GAGE FLUNG DOWN 107

VII. THE TWO PATRIOTISMS 129

VIII. JERUSALEM DELENDA 146

IX. THE LAST STAGE OF THE JOURNEY . . 168

X. JEREMIAH AND GOD 184

APPENDIX I. CHAPTERS XXX AND XXXI . . 211

APPENDIX II. THE COMPOSITION OF THE BOOK OF
JEREMIAH 214

INDEX I. NAMES AND SUBJECTS . . . 217

INDEX II. PASSAGES IN THE BOOK OF JEREMIAH . 221

CHRONOLOGICAL TABLE

B.C.

c. 750. Amos.

c. 740–735. Work of Hosea.

737–700. Work of Isaiah.

722. Capture of Samaria by the Assyrians.

c. 701. Deliverance of Jerusalem from Sennacherib.

698–641. Reign of Manasseh.

646. Beginning of the Decline of Assyria.

639. Accession of Josiah.

626. Call of Jeremiah.

621. Discovery of Law Book.

612. Fall of Nineveh.

608. Death of Josiah at Meggido. Exile of Jehoahaz. Accession of Jehoiakim.

605. Defeat of Necho at Carchemish.

604. Baruch's Roll.

597. Death of Jehoiakim. First Deportation. Accession of Zedekiah.

592–572. Work of Ezekiel, in Babylonia.

588. Revolt of Judah.

586. Capture of Jerusalem by Nebuchadnezzar. Second Deportation.
Murder of Gedaliah. Jeremiah taken to Egypt.

JEREMIAH
AND THE NEW COVENANT

I

"NOT FOR AN AGE
BUT FOR ALL TIME"

THE study of the Bible has often suffered from the fact that its great characters have been regarded as above criticism. The Bible has its villains: Ahab, Haman, Simon Magus, Judas; and its heroes have their dark passages. Abraham, Jacob and David are guilty of actions that all their admirers deplore; this is true even of Paul, and, of course, of Peter. The narratives of such faults have generally been used to inspire us with caution for ourselves, and admiration for the candour of the sacred historians; but they have seldom been allowed to dim the glories of the heroic characters. So with the style of the Biblical writings. It is never admitted to be bad or turgid or confused. If some passage makes bad sense as it stands, the transcriber must bear the blame. The prophets who foretold the Messiah must be as blameless as the warriors who typified Him.

The practice however is dangerous. The zeal defeats its ends. It is better to accept the faults and try to account for them than to pretend that they do not exist. To raise the character to a more than human pedestal is to deprive him of

interest. Even an Aristides will lose his popularity
when he is always called " the Just " ; and no
severer ordeal could be assigned to a writer than
that he should be made a continual theme for
sermons or books of edification. It is small wonder
that while the great men of genius of Greece and
Rome and Italy and our own country number
their lovers by the ten thousand, the splendid and
daring orators and poets of Israel, safely but
regrettably packed away inside what is tradition-
ally known as an inspired book, should be only
known and loved by the thousand or the hundred.

We can imagine how restless these great men
would be in receiving such an ambiguous honour.
That they themselves were inspired, in a quite
intelligible sense of the word, is certain. But to
regard them as removed from the sphere of the
process of criticism and estimation by which we
study other classical writers is really to transfer
them to a sort of limbo or wax-work show, an
act against which they would have protested with
all the force at their command. They were
prepared to be despised and insulted, and even
to be mistaken and deceived ; they could not
bear to be platform favourites, applauded, and
forgotten.[1]

All true appreciation and admiration of the
prophets must rest on the kind of criticism we
expect to be applied to every classic. With men
whose works have so remarkably stood the test of
time and change, we may assume power and genius ;
we must not assume freedom from the faults for
which we are prepared in other writers of dis-

[1] Ezek. xxxiii. 32.

tinction ; nor must we fear the charge of irrever-
ence if we subject to tests, familiar elsewhere,
writings which are introduced to us with the
majestic phrase, " Thus saith the Lord." In our
own day all the conspicuous figures of the past are
being submitted in turn to a process of psychological
as well as literary analysis. Some of their admirers
may already be beginning to feel that this kind of
thing may easily be overdone. But the Biblical
writers cannot and ought not to claim immunity
from the process.

The prophets at all events, as the study of any of
them will show, have given us no large masterpieces
which can be examined as we can examine *King
Lear* or Dante's *Purgatorio* or *The Prelude* or even
Lycidas. Their literary beauties are like the fitful
beauties of the fragments of the Greek lyric poets
or tragedians. But there are other aspects in their
work which we can study. What was the world in
which they lived ? What were their hopes and
fears, their inner conflicts and half-conscious
desires ? Did they accept life as they found it,
or did they defy it ? Which of Hamlet's eternal
alternatives did they choose, to bear their fortune
or to take arms against it ? To approach an answer
to such questions, when we are dealing with any
man capable of writing words which twenty
centuries have refused to abandon, is to arrive at a
better understanding of him, and of ourselves.

Of all the prophets of Israel, we know Jeremiah
the best. This is not merely because he has left
us a larger body of writings than most ; Ezekiel
alone has surpassed him in actual bulk. We know
more about his immediate surroundings. We

possess, in addition to his public addresses, a number of private and self-revealing meditations— a sort of *journal intime* ; and we have also a body of memoirs written by a close friend and admirer. In all this, the parallel with another Jew of the tribe of Benjamin, Saul of Tarsus, is curiously close.

When we put together the materials thus presented, we find a type by no means unfamiliar to us in these later days : the man who is in revolt against society. This is indeed how all the prophets present themselves to us, from Amos to Ezekiel. Popularly supposed to busy themselves with prediction, they really devote their fiery energies to attacks on the ignorance, the futility, the sordid aims and the gross and brutal ideals of their own times. Sometimes we seem to hear the lofty eloquence of a Ruskin, sometimes the vehemence of a street preacher or—shall we say ?—a communist ; sometimes the whirling ferocity of a Nietzsche. Between Nietzsche and Jeremiah, indeed, there is more than one link. Both proclaimed their undying hostility to the world in which they lived ; both edged their denunciations with bitter personal emotions ; both were forced, in order to obey the inner impulse, to steel themselves against tendencies within them which would have led them in a very different direction ; and both possessed a keen sense of beauty and an enormous capacity for suffering. With each of them the ruthless condemnation levelled at the world outside was, at least in part, the result of a perpetual conflict in the spirit within.

On the other hand, the differences between them

are no less illuminating. Nietzsche lived in an intellectual world in comparison with which Jeremiah's was a country village. At Nietzsche's feet were all the treasures of art and literature, ancient and modern ; he knew his way to the heart (or near it) of scholar and musician. For Jeremiah, beauty meant no more than the passage of a bird over the bare hillside, the fresh brown of the newly ploughed soil, or the artless notes of a peasant girl's song. But where Nietzsche saw man, or the super-man, Jeremiah saw God ; where Nietzsche was satisfied to despise the slaves crowded around him, Jeremiah longed for their redemption. Nietzsche was the centre of his own world ; behind all his scorn, his denunciation, his hatred for the Prussian philistines, was a deep longing for supremacy : to impose his own will on his own surroundings and his own future. Jeremiah, with the same passionate resentments, the same violent reaction against personal opposition, learnt to be the servant and the mouthpiece of a power and wisdom infinitely higher than his own, and, restless and perturbed as he was to the end, to find in that wisdom his peace.

To see in his history the record of a long-drawn-out inward conflict is not to surrender to the technique of our modern psycho-analysts. His was a nature made up of oppositions. Conflict was inevitable. Sensitiveness, passion, aloofness ; a mind delighted with simple intimacies and familiar sights, yet repelled and outraged by evils which every one around him could tolerate or defend : such a combination of characteristics was bound to find some relief in compromise or surrender, or else to burn itself out at the last in weariness and strife. In modern times Jeremiah might have redirected his energies as a social reformer. He might have become a Blake or a Cobbett. In his own day, he could only be a prophet, and a prophet of doom. But he was something more. Nietzsche could exult over the society whose weaknesses and pusillanimities he exposed; Jeremiah was one with the men and women he condemned. To pronounce their ruin was to tear at his own heart-strings. A conflict like this could find no end on this side of the grave.

We have spoken of Jeremiah as a prophet. To be a prophet did not only intensify the conflict, but transformed it. For there was in Israel a definite prophetic tradition. Certain convictions, as we can see, might turn a man into a prophet; but for such a man the actual turning-point was not a conviction or an illumination, but a " call." The careers of all the greater prophets begin, as it would seem, with a definite summons by a divine voice. This is certainly true of Isaiah and Ezekiel; it is probably true of Amos and Hosea and Elijah, and of the two great heroes of the past often reputed to be the founders of the prophetic succession, Moses and Samuel. Moreover, the prophet was not left after his call to think out his own propaganda. All his inner experiences were understood to be directly originated by God; so that his addresses were naturally introduced by his repeated, " Thus hath Jehovah said."

A man who prefaced his words in this way was almost sure, in Israel, of serious attention, at least from some part of his audiences; but such a claim has been made far too often to impress, by itself, the student of religious beliefs. Pagan and Christian records are full of these claims; they are found in every continent and in every age. They are so easily put forward by self-confidence, however sincere, and accepted by credulity, however pious, that they immediately raise a prejudice in the mind of the experienced critic. Nothing has been too fantastic, and too immoral, to be promulgated, and received, as a divine message. And the effect on the character of the recipient has generally been unfortunate. Singled out, as he thinks, for so exalted a favour, he grows conceited and over-bearing, intolerant and fanatical. Few indeed are strong enough to bear the weight of infallibility. Even the journals of George Fox, though the community which he founded numbered among its adherents the gentlest and humblest of Christians, weary the reader with the unconscious arrogance of one who is always in the right; and Mohammad, equally sure of the divine illumination, ended by mistaking for heavenly commands (if he did mistake them) the dictates of a rather sordid expediency and self-indulgence.

Yet, from the whole crowd of such mouthpieces of the Divine, the prophets stand out as a distinct class. The reason is that their tradition was not simply psychological but moral. Instead of leading to extravagance and fanaticism, it steadied the excitement of their minds while it narrowed the content of their message. However exuberant may have been the patriotic expectations of their forerunners in Israel, the range of their own

ideas was for the most part confined to three
beliefs : that conduct was alone of real importance
in the eyes of God ; that disobedience to His will
meant destruction ; but that at the last God
would bring back Israel to Himself.

Even more intensely than the other prophets
does Jeremiah concentrate on these three axioms.
The circumstances of the time, especially in his
later years, still further intensified this concentration. They have made his teaching singularly
barren in what may be called new ideas. He has
been accused of adding nothing to the religious
knowledge of the race. The accusation can be
justified ; yet to repeat it is not to condemn the
prophet but to exalt him. For if he brought no
new idea to the common stock of his time, or ours,
he saw every old one with a new clearness and
sublimity. Novelty at best is an ambiguous asset
to the preacher. Even Jesus, if He claimed it on
one occasion, repudiated it on another. Jeremiah
was no theological teacher. He was a man who
took a few convictions to his heart, *non ita dis-
putandi causa, sed ita vivendi*—to live by them,
not to argue about them—as was said of another
serious and ardent thinker. They were subjected to
every kind of strain and of solvent ; to hold them,
as he held them, almost broke his resolution, or
his faith, but they were never given up.

To say this is not to put him on a pinnacle out
of the reach of our criticism or our sympathy.
His character had its share of weaknesses, some
of which attract, while others repel. The one
weakness of which he was never guilty was to
think that God could be bribed or cajoled or

propitiated into unfaithfulness to His own stern demands, or wearied or disgusted into forgetfulness of His own gracious purpose.

Is this all that can be said ? Is there nothing on the other side, nothing that can be called inspiration ? The whole subject of the following chapters may be said to be an attempt to answer this question. Clearly, it cannot be answered off-hand. How shall we decide what part of the prophet's message came from without, and what from within ? And in which realm, the external or the internal, shall we most wisely look for the source of the prophet's inspiration ? We shall indeed endeavour to reach some conclusion at the end of our study ; here we would only say that all criticism of a religious message must concern itself more with its subject-matter, which we can examine, than with its rise and origin, at which we can only guess. Behind Jeremiah's three axioms are three great conceptions : justice, mercy, and humility towards God. He neither created nor discovered them. He would have repudiated such a suggestion with vehemence. Their importance had been expressed in imperishable words long before his call,[1] and they had been known in Israel long before that. They were revealed in the sense in which we can say that the Ten Commandments were revealed, or the institution of marriage, or the law of veracity. And if at last we come to believe that God really did speak to Jeremiah, it will be because the truths which he gave his life to proclaim are among the central truths by which men live, and because the manner

[1] Micah vi. 8.

B

of his proclaiming them shows that a force greater than his own was at work upon him.

Lastly, the question may be raised, Could not others outside Palestine have been so illuminated and inspired ? Why single out Jeremiah and the other Hebrew prophets ? Doubtless others were so inspired ; inspiration is a matter of degree rather than class or race. We only do the Biblical writers disservice if we spend time or ingenuity in asking what they had that no one else ever possessed. But what we can and must assert is that these axioms and conceptions, as we have called them, never found full or adequate expression till the prophets came and voiced them ; that they have never been stated more nobly or clearly than by the prophets ; and that all the writers and preachers who have stated them since, whatever their age or creed, have derived their knowledge of them and their enthusiasm for them, directly or indirectly, from the prophets.

Among such men as these, conspicuous alike in the depth of his feeling, the intensity of his suffering, the wealth of his sympathy, his life-long conflict with opposition and incredulity, and his pathetic and unbroken fidelity to his mission, stands Jeremiah.

In the succeeding chapters an endeavour is made to present what may be called a life of Jeremiah. This is far from easy ; for although, as we have said, we possess more material for Jeremiah than for any other of the prophets (not even excluding Ezekiel), the material is at best scanty, ill-arranged, and often undated ; and it is combined with a great deal which cannot be attributed to the prophet, and with much else which is probably, but not certainly, from some other hand. It is true that we also possess the memoirs of his friend and secretary, Baruch ; these are for the most part dated ; but they only cover comparatively small sections of his life, and raise almost as many questions as they answer.

If, however, in planning out the prophet's biography, we begin with those points that we can regard as practically fixed, we can form conclusions about both his inner and his outer life which will enable us to go forward with reasonable confidence. Interest and admiration will always impel us to advance where caution will bid us hesitate. Neither of these two counsellors must be silenced. If the scholars who have written on Jeremiah had confined themselves to what was beyond the reach of all doubt, their works would be brief indeed. Every attempt to write the life even of Paul or of Jesus must often move in the region of conjecture. The plan of this book excludes any detailed discussion of critical questions ; but in the following pages the reader, it is hoped, will find that reasons are given for any important statements which might seem at all precarious ; and an Appendix has been added, to consider, in a little more detail than is possible in the body of the book, the date of the most important of all the sections in the prophecy.

It is however far more important to read what Jeremiah wrote than what others have written about him. To make this easier, at the head of each chapter are prefixed references to the passages

which appear to fall within the period covered by
the chapter ; and in the body of the chapter these
passages are summarised.[1]

Besides the familiar translations in the Authorised
and Revised Versions, the reader has the choice of
four others. Dr J. E. McFadyen (*Jeremiah in
Modern Speech*, Clarke, 6s.) has very successfully
rendered the poetical sections of the book into
metrical English, Hebrew prose being rendered by
English prose. Dr A. C. Welch (*Jeremiah*, Adult
School Union, 2s. 6d.) offers a prose translation
which is intentionally very colloquial, and the
book is further divided into brief sections, to each
of which a terse but informing introductory
paragraph is prefixed. Dr J. Moffatt (*The Old
Testament ; a New Translation*, vol. ii., Hodder &
Stoughton, 10s.) has produced a very skilful version
which, in many places, is really commentary as well
as translation ; and the larger part of the book is to
be found arranged in chronological order with brief
notes, in Kent's *Sermons, Epistles, and Apocalypses
of Israel's Prophets* (Hodder & Stoughton). The
most useful commentaries on Jeremiah are by
Dr A. S. Peake (2 vols., Century Bible) and
Dr A. W. Streane (Cambridge Bible for Schools).
A very full and suggestive monograph on Jeremiah
has been written by Dr J. Skinner (*Prophecy and
Religion*, Cambridge Press, 12s. 6d.). Nearly forty
years ago Cheyne wrote *Jeremiah, His Life and*

---

[1] These passages include most of what, in the author's opinion,
can be confidently attributed to Jeremiah : but there is a good deal
more included in the canonical Book of Jeremiah which may have
come from him. In several passages there have been extensive
later additions. See pp. 48 *f.* and Appendix II.

Times, a work which, for its vividness and sympathy with the religious life of the prophet, may still be read with very great advantage; and the reader may also consult J. R. Gillies, *Jeremiah*, *The Man and His Message* (Hodder & Stoughton) and W. R. Thomson, *The Burden of the Lord* (Clarke, 6s.). Full references to German literature are given by Peake and Skinner.

II

THE YOUTH AND HIS CALL

c. 626 B.C.

(Jeremiah i.)

To understand a genius we ought to go back to his adolescence. But this is seldom possible. We can trace a great man's history back to his first adventures in his art or activity ; to the " call," perhaps, which first made him conscious of an ideal and a life-long duty of service to it. Yet the real circumstances, the early morning fascination of that call, are apt to be hidden from him, in later life, as from ourselves. Neither he nor we, looking back upon it, can separate the memory of the starting-point on the long journey from the memory of the various experiences brought by the rest of the road. The great man is to us always the great man. We cannot strip him of his later achievements and come to the youth, in whom no one else saw anything remarkable, who hardly knew whether to believe in himself, who had nothing to his credit ; who could not tell, as he looked into the grey mists, where the road would lead (if indeed it was to lead anywhere at all), and who was no more, to his friends and to himself, than an unknown lad from some little Nazareth, the son of a carpenter.

Sometimes indeed we can pick up a hint or

two, or even something more. We can see the small Giotto making his rough sketches on the hillside under a clear Italian sky, with his sheep half-forgotten around him, even while he draws them ; or Mozart, learning to woo, with infant fingers, the old spinet in his father's attic ; or Bach, familiar with music in his melodious home at Eisenach before he was familiar with anything else. Now and then a poet will set himself to tell us of his own childhood. But when Wordsworth describes the boy who skated on Windermere or was haunted by the cataract or beguiled into sleep in the lonely hills or initiated into the deeper secrets of nature, we know that we see the eager lad through maturer eyes. We are looking backward and not forward. At other times we are left to reconstruct as best we can the message of crowded chaffering streets and solemn colonnades and far-voyaging ships by the quays at Tarsus, or of Warwickshire lanes and deer trotting across the glades in the park at dawn. What we cannot do is to recapture the wonder and the wild surmise of the world which held up one beckoning finger, while the other lay, so to speak, on the lip, and hinted at a secret which only the years could reveal—which might need a lifetime before its full glories could be disclosed, or might be told, hurriedly yet rapturously, just before premature death came to end all. For us, to think of Shakespeare and Keats in their boyhood is to think of the continuity, the slowly maturing power of the one, and the quick draining of a jewelled cup —was it drained ?—by the other ; of all, in short, that was mercifully hidden from their own eyes.

Is the attempt to do anything else worth while ? It must be, if we are to live the great man's life over again with him. We cannot grow old with him if we have not been young with him first. But there is another reason for making the attempt. The scenes and experiences of childhood have the first chance with us. It is not simply that they provide a store of memories, held more or less closely in after years, which, even when no longer consciously recalled, live and work in what we conveniently call the sub-conscious. Nor is it that in childhood are formed those complexes which give their tone and colour to all the loves and hates, the hopes and fears, of later life. More than this ; these experiences mould the imaginative world of the grown man. They form the background against which he builds up the episodes of his career. Desire and disappointment, failure and success, come to us all. But how different their effect if they are, as it were, projected against an open country-side where storm is always sooner or later followed by serene weather and there is always some busy and varied life to be watched in hedge-row or field or sky, or against the crowded slums, let us say, of a Russian city, where every one gets in every one else's way, and where, amidst brutal ignorance and debauchery, aspiration can at best become a transfigured acquiescence in misery.

As it happens, there is no great difficulty in picturing the surroundings of the youthful Jeremiah. Anathoth, his father's home, was a village some three or four miles to the north-west of Jerusalem, perched between two and three thousand feet above sea-level. To the east, the country fell, in a succession of precipices (even the modern traveller will call them nothing else) to the deep trench of the Jordan, here lower than sea-level by nearly another three hundred feet. To climb from Jericho to Anathoth was like climbing from Wasdale to the top of Scafell Pike. The Jordan Valley, compared with Wasdale, was a veritable tropical jungle; but as one struggled up the stony ravines to Anathoth, one reached a long tableland, where the farmer had to fight with a recalcitrant soil for every foot of cultivable and terraced ground. Though so near to the capital, the village looked northward. The city itself was half hidden by the Mount of Olives; but away to the north the rolling wind-swept slopes led to Gibeah of Saul and Ramah and Bethel and the site of the ancient national shrine, long since cruelly destroyed, of Shiloh. Political fortunes had joined Benjamin, to which Anathoth properly belonged, to the Kingdom of Judah; but the old tribal sympathies were still with Ephraim. Samaria, where the proud and restless kings of Israel had reigned less than a century ago, was only twenty-five miles, a single good day's journey, to the north.

In the reign of David, the two priests, Zadok and Abiathar, had done as much as the great captains Joab and Abishai to uphold the king's romantic throne. But the young Solomon, following, as it would seem, his father's advice, determined to get rid of his father's best friends. Joab was murdered, Abiathar was allowed to retire into insignificance at Anathoth. Here his descendants continued to reside. The priest

Hilkiah, whose family owned land in Anathoth three hundred years later, may have been one of these. What his duties as priest were it is hard to tell. Did he take his turn in " doing duty " at the Temple in Jerusalem, as Zacharias did in the years before the birth of Jesus, or was he left by the " established clergy " of the Temple to conduct the more modest worship of the shrine at Anathoth ? The latter is the more probable ; for, as we know was the case a little later, there would naturally be jealousy between the priests of the city and the country ; and there would in any case be little love lost between the succession of Zadok and the descendants of the dispossessed and ejected Abiathar. Religious and family affinities probably pointed, with as much clearness as did the lie of the country, away from Jerusalem and towards the hills of Ephraim.

Into such surroundings was born, in the middle of the seventh century before Christ, Hilkiah's son, Jeremiah ; and it is not hard to picture the world which surrounded the child's early years. The England of half a millennium before Christ would be quite unrecognisable by us ; but to the traveller in Palestine, site after site of those far-off days can be identified with considerable ease. The same villages (very often with the names hardly changed) crown the hill-tops ; the same drama of farm and field and sheepfold is carried through each year ; the house-wife pursues the same tasks as her long-forgotten ancestress, and the great business of eating, drinking, working, bearing and rearing children, and sliding down into old age, goes on still as it has gone on for ages.

Only in two respects have changes come. Centuries of misrule and oppression, coupled perhaps with gradual changes of climate and diminution of rainfall, have given the country a look of barrenness and poverty which it cannot have known in Biblical times; and modern commercial ventures, European engineers, and, later, the British occupation, have, for good or ill, begun their work of development. Yet, in spite of both these changes, Palestine is still largely what it was. The traveller who looks at the country with a boy's eyes can see what the boy Jeremiah saw and loved: the sudden burst of vegetation with the spring rains and the returning warmth; the long hot dry days and rustic merrymakings of harvest; the break of the summer's heat with the " early " showers of autumn; the flight of the migrating stork; the sheep straggling over the hills or gathering at some trodden pool at evening; the yelp of a jackal or the roar of a lion from a ravine down below; the breaking of the untilled ground, the threshing and the winnowing and, later, the labour of the oil-press and the wine-vat.

There was plenty for the Hebrew lad to see, and to learn. Each village was more or less independent economically. It made its own domestic utensils; it wove its own cloth as it grew and prepared its own food. All that was needed for his life the boy would see produced at his own door. Not more than two miles away ran the North Road from Jerusalem to Bethel and Shechem. It was not one of the great trade and military roads of the world, like the coast-road from Gaza to Joppa and the Plain of Esdraelon. But peasants from the central hills, merchants from Damascus, and envoys and soldiers from Assyria passed one another along it, and helped Jeremiah to feel how rich and varied was the world he lived in. In the village, each family clung to its own ancestral lands, and prayed to continue to live under its own vine and fig-tree. But bad times would come ; money to carry on the farm or to buy seed-corn would have to be borrowed ; sometimes an unfortunate farmer would have to sell himself and his family to pay his debts ; and the Hebrew slave would work in the fields which he once had owned.

Though the amount of money involved was so much less, the power of money was as great and as tyrannous as it can be to-day ; and the " usurer " was loathed as he was loathed in the Middle Ages, or in present-day India. Then, too, there was the village " gate," where disputed claims were arbitrated and quarrels settled and news discussed ; there were the festivals of sowing and reaping in which all could happily take their part ; there were the rumours of events beyond the hills—the death of a prince, a Bedouin foray, or the movements of those dreaded Scythians who had terrified other lands and might devastate Judah. There were the weeks of scanty fare in late winter, the plenty of the early April harvest, ushered in traditionally by the Passover, and the great events of marriage and birth and death, which did not belong to this or that family only but to the whole village.

Here was material in plenty for the education of the lad. But was there anything more organised ? He would certainly learn to read and write.

His father, the priest, would see to that. More important, he would learn the essentials of the religion of his fathers. This was largely a matter of what we should call history ; and it was not to be learnt from books, but from oral traditions—stories told round the hearth or the camp-fire. What these traditions were we can see pretty clearly from the examples of them preserved in what are known as the Jahvist and Elohist documents of the Pentateuch and the historical books, tales rather loosely connected with one another, but each of them with a more or less definite form (like the incidents in the Synoptic Gospels), and capable of expansion or modification by different reciters or in different places and (unlike the Gospels) going back to a dim and hoary antiquity. Their subjects were the grace, the guidance, and the wrath of Jahveh,[1] as manifested to hero or prophet or farmer in the past, or as influencing the destinies of the whole nation.

Possibly, too, Jeremiah would have access, through his father, to the annals or more formal contemporary records of each year, kept at the court. As time went on, he would be introduced to another literature, that of the prophets. Just about a century before his birth, Amos had startled the worshippers at Bethel, then one of the chief sanctuaries of the Northern Kingdom, by his grim

[1] The form Jahveh, if it is pronounced *Yahweh*, represents fairly well what was in all probability the old Hebrew sound of the divine name.   It is rendered in our Bibles as " the LORD " ; and, at least in many places, it suggests, more distinctly than the other term " God," the divine power which was specially interested in the nation of Israel (*cf*. Exod. iii. 15 ; Amos iii. 1, 2).

predictions of a swiftly coming ruin, and his words, either by himself, or by some circle of friends, had been written down. He was followed by Hosea, some few years later, and Hosea, as we shall see, made a deep impression on Jeremiah. Meanwhile, in Jerusalem, Isaiah had been prophesying, and Micah; and collections of these prophetic utterances were being made, though the reader could not always be sure either of their authors or of their occasions, and indeed was seldom very interested in either question.

In this literature, the lad would find clearly, perhaps more clearly than he could find elsewhere, an insistence on a certain moral tradition, of straightforward, honest, and kindly conduct, as the most acceptable thing in the eyes of Jahveh; the prompt payment of wages; the refusal to press an advantage against a poorer man; and a high ideal of general good-will, self-control, and chastity. This, he would there learn, constituted the special worship of Jahveh, and had done so from the days when Jahveh had first revealed himself on Sinai. In his insistence on all this, Israel's God was quite unlike the gods of all other nations. But the boy would learn other lessons which must have seemed strangely inconsistent with all this. He would learn that Jahveh had to be approached, if at all, by sacrifice; that he would only listen to the worshipper who brought him gifts; and that these gifts could only be accepted under conditions of ritual cleanliness. The altars where these gifts were to be offered were to be found at special and " holy " places and shrines; on the eminences which could be seen on all sides ; under the clumps of trees which generally crowned them ; or by some spring or stream in a valley. Often the shrine was associated with some story of Jahveh or of a patriarch— particularly so at places like Bethel or Gilgal. Every family had its annual or seasonal celebrations, half religious worship, half family feast. But at the greater shrines there were also other and darker rites : the sacrifice of human beings, children or adolescents; and the presence of women, known as "holy" or consecrated to the god, who were expected to prostitute themselves to the worshipper, as if religion were nothing more than a kind of sympathetic magic, very pleasant and alluring, to ensure fertility and bountiful crops.

And such, indeed, in one form it undoubtedly was. In fact, whether the young Jeremiah would at first recognise this or not, there were really two religions in Israel ; the religion of the prophets or of Sinai, as we may call it, and the religion of the shrines and of the Baalim, their lords (Baal="lord") and protectors. And, as Jeremiah could not but see, the second was the exact opposite of the first. Of the moral demands of the first, the second made and could make nothing ; while all that it cultivated was expressly and fundamentally opposed to the rigorous ideals of the first. Possibly, too, he was conscious of another opposition, one of which his father would not keep him in ignorance. Beyond all the other shrines stood out in importance the temple at Jerusalem. In relation to the rest, the temple naturally shared in the prestige of the capital. It possessed an imposing grandeur unknown anywhere else in the Southern Kingdom. It had always been connected with the court since its ceremonial dedication by Solomon. At the same time, the general traditions of its worship seem to have been higher than those of most of the local shrines, and less touched by purely Canaanite influences. Until the last fevered years of the city's existence, we know nothing of any image worship within its precincts. We also read of more than one reformation of the ritual there, under Asa, Jehoshaphat, and Hezekiah. The result of all this would be to differentiate between the worship of the shrines, at Anathoth and elsewhere, and *the* shrine at Jerusalem; but this differentiation would not raise the temple or displace the local shrines in the affections of the peasants of the countryside.

To the Hebrews, religion and history went together. But neither religion nor history was a matter of simple brooding over the past, or of discussing the place of ritual in relation to conduct. At every stage in the nation's life, and never more so than in the seventh century, religion had to follow the course of history through pressing anxieties and vivid fears. Jeremiah's birth occurred at the close of the reign of Manasseh, a period of long and prosperous peace. All through that reign, save perhaps for one instance to be mentioned presently, Manasseh had maintained a policy of subservience to Assyria. Judah, indeed, as a regular tributary, had been really a part of the far-flung Assyrian Empire ever since Ahaz had put himself under Assyria's protection nearly a century before, in 735 B.C. And never had that

empire been prouder or more glorious than when
Manasseh reigned as an Assyrian vassal in Jerusalem.
Esar-haddon, who came to the throne in 681,
had restored the Assyrian power in Babylon,
clearing out the Chaldeans who had disputed
lower Mesopotamia with him; faced the pressure
of the Medes and Scythians in the North-West,
and bought over the Scythian chieftains into
alliance with himself; received the submission of
both Tyre and Sidon, thus establishing himself
firmly on the Mediterranean; and then had carried
his arms into Egypt. In the midst of these labours
he died, to be succeeded in 660 by Ashur-bani-pal,
who in a brilliant series of campaigns conquered
Egypt and set up its king, Psamtik, by a bold
stroke, on the throne, as his vassal; destroyed the
empire of Elam for ever; installed himself as
king of Babylon; and drove away to the North
the Cimmerians by his army in Syria. No other
worlds remained for Assyria to conquer; and in
642 Ashur-bani-pal celebrated a triumph un-
equalled for its splendour. Then the strength of
the old lion suddenly began to give way. The
stages of the decline are somewhat obscure. Assyria
did not chronicle her weakness as she chronicled
her strength. But, for the next thirty years,
that decline is the dominant fact in the history of
Western Asia.

In the year after Ashur-bani-pal's triumph,
when Jeremiah would be about three or four
years old, Manasseh died. Outwardly calm as
his reign had been, there was movement enough
under the surface from the beginning. Hezekiah,
his father, after some indecision, had made up his

c

mind to risk opposition to Assyria. He had come
to an understanding with Babylon and had headed
a coalition of Palestinian states ; and though his
own territory, like that of his allies, had suffered
severely, Jerusalem by a miracle had remained
safe. Independence in politics meant independence in religion ; and the reformation which we
have already mentioned, while it strengthened
the influence of the capital over the now sadly
impoverished province, brought to an end a great
deal of Assyrian or semi-Assyrian worship which
had come in under Ahaz. But, with Manasseh,
all this was changed. Making his peace with
Assyria, he introduced the worship of Assyrian
deities on a much larger scale than before. The
later Hebrew chroniclers spoke with horror of the
worship of the sun and of the queen of heaven.
Strong protests were made, both on religious
and political grounds. But Manasseh ruthlessly
stamped out all opposition in blood. Assyria was
to have no more ground for suspecting the loyalty
of Judah. Even Manasseh, however, may not
have been always faithful. The movements in
the countries round Judah which preceded Assyria's
final supremacy there would be a sore temptation
to him to withhold his payments. The obscure
narrative in Chronicles of Manasseh's captivity in
Babylon,[1] perhaps, rests on the fact that Manasseh
chose his time to repeat the experiment of Hezekiah ;
possibly, too, he was dallying with Egypt. He
was in consequence carried off to Babylon, and
then allowed, in chastened mood, when the Assyrian
power was firmer than ever, to return. Such a

[1] 2 Chron. xxxiii. 11 f.

proceeding would at all events be consistent with the statemanship of Ashur-bani-pal. If he could place an ex-rebel, Psamtik, on the throne of Egypt, why not allow Manasseh to go back to Jerusalem?

Manasseh was succeeded by his son Amon. In two years Amon was murdered. The narrative in Kings sets the guilt upon a conspiracy of his "servants."[1] Evidently there was a party in the court itself which opposed the policy of Manasseh; and with Amon on the throne, they felt strong enough to enforce their own ideas. Significantly enough, the prophet Zephaniah, who declared against Manasseh's whole religious policy in the reign of Josiah, was a prince of the blood royal, and a cousin of Manasseh himself. Perhaps there were others in equally high places who felt with him. But the murder was quickly avenged. The conspirators were themselves put to death by a rising of "the people of the land." The mass of the population, it would seem, had no desire for risky attempts at independence, and as little enthusiasm for religious reform. Amon's son, Josiah, a boy of eight years old, was crowned. What the immediate sequel was, we can only guess; but some twenty years later we shall find Josiah surrounded by a group of men firmly opposed to all the ideals of Manasseh. The "people of the land" might for a moment seize the helm; they did not succeed in setting the course.

Those events could not fail of their repercussion in Anathoth. The reforms would not be popular there; for an integral part of those reforms was the attempt to supersede or destroy the worship

[1] 2 Kings xxi. 23.

of the local shrines and to confine all religious
services to the temple in the capital. It is true,
we do not actually know of the existence of a
shrine there; but the constant references in the
prophets to shrines throughout the whole of
Judah make it very probable; and the later history
of Jeremiah confirms it. The reaction under
Manasseh would naturally be welcomed here,
and the popular party which avenged the murder
of Amon would have its members or sympathisers
in this and many another village. What the
attitude of Hilkiah himself would be we cannot
tell. We only know that in later years Jeremiah
was somewhat closely connected with the statesmen
who supported Josiah, and Hilkiah and " the people
of the land " may have been on opposite sides.
It is more interesting to ask how the change would
strike the priest's young son as he came to understand what had happened. At the accession of
Josiah he was probably about five or six years
old.[1]

He grew up with an intense love for his country
home and the simple open-air life of which it was
the centre. This is clearly shown by the language
and imagery of his poems. Unlike Isaiah, he
always writes as one who, at least in thought and
imagination, lives in the country. He cannot

---

[1] We have no information as to the date of his birth. But he
was still quite young when his " call " took place in 626, and it
was at least some years after this that he made up his mind that he
was not to marry. As marriage generally took place while the
bridegroom was still a young man, he could not be more than
twenty in 626, and we should place his birth therefore about 645,
at the end of Manasseh's reign.

keep away from birds and animals, flowers and crops. To the end, his language is the simple direct speech of one who has always been at home with nature. Like many another nature-lover, he was shy and diffident ; yet he was no recluse ; he was equally at home in the life of the village. His references to the transient sorrows and household cares and joys of the village remind one of Wordsworth's zest in the simple Cumberland gatherings in which he would join so heartily in his college vacations. The busy sound of the housewife's mill, the cry of the ploughman to his team, and the " voice of the bridegroom and the bride " were ever in his ears when he thought of some ideally happy state. And if we may judge from his later writings, there were deep contrasts in his nature as well. Receptive, yet intense and self-centred ; open-eyed, yet much given to reflection and brooding ; with strong æsthetic susceptibilities, yet determined to call even the grossest things by their right names ; self-controlled, yet subject to quick revulsions of feelings and outbursts of passionate indignation ; he had the clear moral intuitions of a generous and high-minded boy. He would not see, or make, fine distinctions. Faced, as he could not but be faced, by the clash between the religion of cultus and the religion of morality, there is not a sign that he hesitated between them for a moment. Sacerdotal as all the traditions of his family might be, cultus made no appeal to him. He was all on the side of conduct. He was a young Puritan. He could have understood the author of *Il Penseroso*, and even of *L'Allegro* ; but he would have been far more at home with

Lycidas. There is much to show that he came
early under the spell of Hosea. Hosea, too, was
a Puritan ; but not a Puritan of the type at which
we smile in Shakespeare's comedies or frown with
Sir Walter Scott ; nor even like his own predecessor Amos, a crag on a rocky hill-top, " tempest-
buffeted, citadel-crowned." His was a tender,
emotional nature, reminding us of the chivalrous
Colonel Hutchinson and of Milton himself ; and
the very intensity of his convictions appears to
have been born in the midst of a heartrending
emotional experience.

Again, like Hosea, Jeremiah did not see in cultus
simply an empty ritual, or the ministrations of
" blind mouths " that scarce know how to hold
the shepherd's crook. It had, as we have seen,
a darker side. It meant sexuality, licence, debauchery. With all the " April blood " of youth
in his veins, Jeremiah saw continually the sights
that would tempt colder men than he. Hosea
had taught him the dangerous lesson of thinking
of religion in terms of sex. The old untarnished
religion of the desert was to him the love of a
young bride for her husband. The syncretism of
the rites of Canaan had been infidelity and fornica-
tion. The long-suffering of Jahveh to the nation's
sins, the deliverance from the consequences of
its erratic and wilful foreign policy, had been the
yearning love of the deserted husband. What
wonder if the contest between flesh and spirit
became for Jeremiah a kind of obsession, and if
over the whole life around him he felt the taint
of physical impurity. " The times were out of
joint." Had he lived a thousand years later, he

might have renounced all and taken refuge in a hermit's cell.

But he could not do this. He had to live on at Anathoth, with the priest his father. We can imagine the hours of solitary thought that would be forced upon him by this inner conflict. He was already confronting what was to be the long tragedy of his life ; a nature that craved friendship and affection driven in upon itself, with no one to sympathise or understand. Did he ever suspect that there was a way out of the impasse—a way against which all that was human in his nature would shrink and protest ? " Hosea found his way out in his prophetic mission of appeal and denunciation to his people. What if I, Jeremiah, am to be a prophet too ? " If such a thought ever came, we can understand how he would thrust it aside. Yet how naturally, to such a youth, it would come ; and once there, how naturally it would return, and more importunately for every time that it was suppressed.

This is mere conjecture ; yet conjecture which psychology renders highly probable. But we now reach solid fact. In 626, when Josiah was about twenty years old, the aged Ashur-bani-pal died. The death of the Assyrian king had always been the signal for political excitement and adventure ; more than ever now, when Assyria herself was clearly growing old and exhausted. News reached Palestine of fresh attacks on the empire by the Medes and the Scythians. And the party of independence in Jerusalem, now presumably growing stronger, would see a new hope. Movement, excitement, was everywhere. Was some great world-shaking event at hand? Jeremiah would feel the influences of the time. If there had been conflict before, it would now inevitably be intensified. And for him, at any rate, the great moment came. He received his "call" to be a prophet of Jahveh.

He has left us an account of the experience in a strangely concise yet moving story (chap. i.). But if we are to do justice to it, we should pause for a moment to recollect the other instances of a "call," which indeed Jeremiah must have known as well as we know them ourselves. More than a century before, Isaiah, a high-born youth of Jerusalem, had heard his call in the Temple. Perhaps at some solemn festival which celebrated Jahveh's enthronement, when incense filled the air and half veiled the pillars of the shrine and the stately vestments of the celebrants, he had fallen into an ecstasy or trance, and had become aware of Jahveh himself in the Temple, with winged and burning heavenly figures around him. Trembling and distraught (for how could one see Jahveh, and not die?) he had cried out. But one of the figures touched his lips with a glowing stone from the altar. He heard a divine voice calling for a messenger; he found himself responding and receiving a message to deliver: a message of destruction and woe.

Isaiah's predecessor Amos has given us an account of four distinct but closely related experiences which may well have been the prelude to the rest of his ministry. Each is introduced by the words, "Thus did Jahveh show me." First, Amos was shown a plague of locusts devouring the crops.

He cries out horror-stricken for mercy on the country, and the prayer is granted. Next, he sees a destructive fire. Again he cries for mercy; and again the prayer, he understands, is granted. Next he sees a plumb-line hanging against an uneven wall; and Jahveh tells him that Israel is like the wall, and like it must fall to the ground. Now he no longer asks for mercy. And last, he sees a basket of ripe fruit. This does not, of itself, suggest doom of any kind; but the word for *fruit* is almost identical in sound with the word for *end*; and Amos is told that the end is come for the nation, and ruin is inevitable. There is nothing in any one of these experiences to imply a direct summons to preach. But we also learn, from the prophet's words to Amaziah, the priest at Bethel who heard his actual announcement of the ruin thus foretold, that he was not a member of any professional guild of prophets, but that Jahveh had taken him from his usual occupation in Judah and had sent him on his mission to Israel. We are not informed as to the time of these events or as to their relation to one another; but what seems at least probable is that on four separate occasions Amos saw something which revealed to him an inner and very sombre significance. On the first two occasions, he appears to have had a vision which filled him with horror; but the horror faded with the vision, and to his relief he was left with the conviction that Israel would escape. On each of the last two, after an interval in which perhaps he recognised the general demoralisation more clearly, it was a simple everyday object that he saw; but it suggested to him a thought

of horror which, now, did not pass. At some
other time, before or after, or even perhaps as a
result of these sights, he became aware that he
was to be Jahveh's spokesman; Jahveh " took
him." [1]

This was a very different affair from Isaiah's
call. The peasant from the hills of Judah knew
little of the world of the young aristocrat. But
the two prophets were alike in one important
respect. They were both conscious of maintaining
a colloquy with Jahveh. Isaiah, after he is prepared
by the seraph, hears Jahveh's question and answers
it. Then he in his turn asks a question and is
answered. Amos is asked what he sees, replies,
and hears Jahveh's comment, and in the first two
instances ventures successfully, like Abraham in the
old story, upon expostulation. Have we here to
do with an ecstasy ? This is probable as regards
Isaiah; possible at least as regards the first two
experiences of Amos. But to admit this leaves
untouched a still more important question. What
are we to understand by the words, " Jahveh
said to me " ? Devotees in every age and in many
different religions have professed to hear the voice
of their god. Both Amos and Isaiah tell us again
and again later that they heard Jahveh's words.
Indeed, all that they say they appear to attribute
to Jahveh. The importance of the prophetic
work so begun cannot be exaggerated ; but much
of what is attributed to Jahveh can hardly be
held by us to be the utterance of eternal and
unchanging truth and foreknowledge and love.
The psychological problem is simpler. Ecstasy

[1] Amos vii., viii.

is a vague and ambiguous term. But the two men were clearly sure that something foreign to their ordinary consciousness made itself explicit, convincing them of a duty which was to transform their lives, and of a coming event that would transform the nation around them.

This long discussion has been necessary to enable us to understand Jeremiah's experience; and to that we now return. As he relates it, it had three moments or stages. The first is told with striking simplicity. There was nothing in it that could constitute a vision. Jahveh told him that he had been marked out as a prophet from his birth. He replies, " I am but a youth; I cannot speak." Jahveh bids him merely obey and have no fear. With that, Jahveh "touches his mouth." " See, I place my words in thy mouth; and I give thee authority over the nations, to pluck up and to break down, and to destroy and to overthrow; to build and to plant."

Then there comes, as it would seem, an interval. And now Jahveh speaks again. " What dost thou see ? " (Amos had been asked the same question.) " An almond tree " (an " early-waker," as the Hebrews called it, marking how it blossomed long before the winter sleep was past). " And I," Jahveh replied, " am waking over my people to perform my word." What was that word ? Jeremiah was soon to discover it. Again Jahveh asked him, " What dost thou see ? " " A boiling kettle, facing the North." [1] " And from the

[1] The precise interpretation of the words is obscure; but it is clear that something in the kettle's position made Jeremiah think of the North.

North," was the reply, " do I bring destruction on all the nations ; all the kings of the North will set their thrones before the gate of Jerusalem. Speak thou what I shall bid thee. Thou shalt be a wall of bronze against all the powers of thy country ; but my protection will never fail thee."

What lies behind all this ? We can hardly help comparing it with another call, on the road to Damascus. Of this we have three accounts, one indirectly and two directly from Paul himself. And we may well suspect that Paul read into his memories of what then took place some of his later discoveries of what was implied by the actual commission. Not so with Jeremiah. For he is told nothing of his duties [1] that we do not find him reproducing at once. And further, the naive suggestion of a sort of general durbar outside the walls of Jerusalem, and the commission to tear down and to build up all the nations, though it might suit a youth's eager anticipations of what a prophet might have to see and do, was not borne out in Jeremiah's subsequent career. Whether he wrote down his account immediately or not, it bears the stamp of authenticity. Had he then a vision of Jahveh ? What, if so, did he see ? He gives no such description as would remind us of Isaiah, still less of Ezekiel. And the almond tree and the kettle no more suggest a vision than Amos' plumb-line or basket of fruit. What then of the touch of Jahveh's hand ? That, if taken literally, is much more startling than the approach

---

[1] Save for the two words, " to build and to plant " (i. 10). If they are genuine, and there is no valid reason for doubting them, they have left no trace in what immediately follows.

of Isaiah's seraph. But need it, or, with a Hebrew, could it, be so taken ? It is surely enough to suppose that Jeremiah felt or imagined (are the two quite distinct ?) a touch, in that moment of excitement, upon his mouth. How else could he describe it than as he did ? But however we interpret this, we recognise, as with the earlier prophets, a colloquy between two voices, one of hesitation, the other of conviction ; one of the familiar, the other of the new and transforming.

Was the second voice, then, entirely new ? To his waking consciousness, undoubtedly. But what lay beneath ? We can only hazard a guess. Yet we have seen how such a youth as Jeremiah must have brooded over the past and the future alike. He knew how the "call" had come to Amos and Isaiah. He had learnt from them that Jahveh's will was unchangeable, and his word an unsleeping power. And since, as Isaiah at least had taught him, and as he could not but feel, destruction must come, whence could it come but from the North, that dread region from which all invading armies had swept down on Palestine, and from which, perhaps, an old eschatological tradition had looked for the crisis that was to come at the last ? But before, all had been vague and fluctuating. Now it was fixed and definite. Before, he had thought of possibilities, and perhaps pushed them into the shade. Now he knew that he was chosen to proclaim that evil was rampant ; that doom was surely on its way ; and he knew that though he shrank and trembled, he would be kept safe till his work was done.

And as a result of all this, Jeremiah was left

with four convictions. Whatever else he meant by the words " Jahveh said to me," he meant that he now held something which he could never doubt. And all four convictions came to him at the beginning of the great experience; what followed the sight of the almond tree and the kettle (curiously trivial starting - places for so profound a movement) only deepened the impression. First,[1] he was in the grip of a divine power, deliberately selected by it and equipped. He had been picked out ; he could not help himself. The most rigid of Calvinists could not have gone beyond the assurance of the lad of Anathoth. Secondly, he was doomed to loneliness. How different his fate from that of the official prophets, who lived and worked in companies, and who, from the days of Zedekiah the son of Chenaanah,[2] or of Samuel himself, had voiced the group-mind and the public opinion, more or less reputable, of their time. With these " popular journalists " (if the anachronism may be pardoned) he was to have nothing in common.

Thirdly, he was to be in perpetual opposition. His was to be the role of Cassandra, predicting misery to incredulous or deaf ears. Only a bare hint was given him, at least at this stage, of any word of guidance, of comfort or of forgiveness, that he would have to utter. It was the equip-

---

[1] First in time as well as in importance. This was so with Isaiah, and, probably, with Amos. Analogy at all events would suggest that if Amos had arranged his material as an autobiography, he would have begun his book with vii. 14-15, vii. 1-7, and viii. 1, 2.

[2] 1 Kings xxii. 11.

ment of Amos; and, indeed, Isaiah at his call knew as little of the more positive elements in his future teaching. But Jeremiah could support even this, because of the fourth conviction, that as Jahveh's spokesman he had Jahveh's authority. He was himself set over the nations; he was to root them up and pluck them down. And all their violence and hate would break on him in vain.

A strange stern part for the eager, open-hearted priest's son to play. Stranger still, had he known the discoveries he was to make and the agonising struggles through which he was to pass. But the words, once heard, could never become unspoken. Nearly a hundred years later, we have the picture of another " chosen vessel," who heard the words, " Behold my servant, whom I uphold; I will put my spirit upon him." He was to bring judgment and deliverance to the nations rather than ruin; and he was not to cry or lift up his voice in the streets. But the two were alike in what their mission entailed, contempt and persecution and death; alike also in the simple and direct intercourse with Jahveh which led them through perplexity and despair and turned defeat itself into something more splendid than victory. And they were alike in their relation to one of the greatest conceptions in the whole field of revelation, the conception of the Covenant. Jeremiah, at one of the most tense moments of his life, knew that God's supreme gift would be a new Covenant. The " servant " was himself to be the " Covenant " of the people.

III

" THE TIMES ARE OUT OF JOINT "
626–621 B.C.

ii. 2-4 (p. 46) ; ii. 5-12 (p. 49) ; ii., 29-37 ; iii. 1-5, 19-25 ; iv. 1-4 (pp. 50 f.) ; v. 1-14, 20-31 ; vi. 6-21 (p. 52 f.) ; iv. 5-8, 13-17, 22-26, 18-22, 23-26, 27-31 ; vi. 1-5 (pp. 56 ff.).

WE must now imagine the young prophet waiting for his first message. He knows, in general, what its substance will be. But until the actual words have come, he must be silent. For whatever we may think of the prophet as a psychical phenomenon, and however he might think of himself, he was Jahveh's mouthpiece, only to speak when inspired or " breathed into." With the memory of his call upon him, he could not but look into the world around him with new eyes. The sins of the society in which a man lives are a much more poignant thing to him when he may find himself denouncing the sinners to their face in a few days ; and foreign politics transform themselves for one who is bidden to affect the fate of the nations.

In the political turmoil, too, that broke out on the death of Ashur-bani-pal, one question was becoming of absorbing interest. Assyria was evidently declining ; Egypt was secure in her independence. What was to be the attitude of Judah to Egypt ? Should she transfer her submission from the East to the South-West ? Or

40

should she, too, aim at such independence as she might be able to snatch ? Clearly, words from Jahveh at such a time as this would be of no small import.

The man who received and uttered Jahveh's word was called a prophet or " Nabi." But it was not through the " Nabi " alone that Jahveh's purpose might be discovered. Indeed, every Hebrew believed that the future might be discovered without any reference to Jahveh at all. Persons possessed of clairvoyant powers have been known in every age and every grade of civilisation. It was as natural for the contemporaries of these clairvoyants in Israel, and for themselves, as for our own ancestors, to believe in the existence of " familiar spirits," who could reveal the unknown or perform what was for human beings impossible. These persons—" mediums," as we should call them to-day—were discountenanced by the stricter religious traditions of Israel ; though Saul, who helped to put them down, had recourse to them himself, when a fate like Macbeth's was closing round him. On the other hand, it was perfectly legitimate to " enquire from Jahveh " about the future. The information so needed could be gained from the sacred lot,[1] by a dream, by some sign in nature (like the sound of an army on the march heard in the trees), or perhaps by a direct response from the minister of Jahveh. Samuel indeed was not thought to be above being ready

---

[1] The priest's "ephod" was apparently a bag which contained the two sets of stones, known as " urim " and " thummim," by which the future could be divined. It seems to have been hung up in the shrine when not actually worn by the priest (1 Sam. xxi. 9).

D

to reveal lost property for a small fee; while David, like many other military leaders, was anxious to be supernaturally assured of success. The functions discharged in Greece by the oracle at Delphi, and even such scruples as those of Nicias, were quite familiar in Palestine. The only difference was that to the good Israelite the future was in the hands of Jahveh, and could only be learnt from him.

But the prophets were not oracles or oracular men. Originally, as is well known, they were religious devotees, or ecstatics. They were looked on with a certain amount of awe, for ecstasy implied supernatural possession. But they were held in no special repute.[1] In time, however, their position improved, and, in the Northern Kingdom at least, bands of prophets had a recognised place in connexion with the royal court. They reflected, moreover, the struggles between the purist and the syncretistic elements in religion. Ahab and Jezebel, as we gather, maintained large numbers of prophets who saw no opposition between Jahveh and the Baals; other prophets, who would have nothing to do with the Baals, were hunted down. And each party allowed, however grudgingly, the possession of the spirit of Jahveh to the other.

The prophets, however, did not all of them act in bands. From the time of David onwards, individual prophets appeared, to announce, as well as to foretell, Jahveh's will: Nathan, Ahijah, Jehu the son of Hanani, Micaiah, and others whose

[1] People were surprised that the son of such a respectable landowner as Kish could join their number even temporarily (1 Sam. x. 11 f., xix. 24).

names are not mentioned. Prediction, indeed, though doubtless of chief interest to most of their hearers, was confined to the announcement of what Jahveh was going to bring about for his own purposes—purposes which were always connected with the moral aspect of the conduct of the nation or its rulers. The individual prophets, like the older " gangs," often embodied some element of the incalculable, both in their appearance and their actions. Their enemies accused them either of disturbing society or of being mad. They could not help themselves. Their own countrymen saw in them men possessed by the spirit of Jahveh—this, of course, was not inconsistent with either of the charges just quoted ; foreigners called them men of God, that is, persons gifted with super-natural powers and impulses.[1]

Gradually, what they did became less and less important than what they said. The earlier prophets had impressed their public by the strange and even wild expression of their excitement, whether they chose to explain it or not. The later prophets, even when they were impelled to curious and outlandish acts, placed little or no stress on anything but their spoken words. They were orators. As far as our information goes, the whole prophetic activity of Amos and Hosea and Micah consisted in their speeches, and only once did Isaiah attract attention in any other way (chap. xx. 2). But to speak of them as orators is not to credit them with the flowing style and regular speech of the platform or the pulpit. The effect which they produced was rather that of the Greek

[1] 1 Kings xvii. 17-24.

rhapsodists. Naturally, they spoke to persuade;
they were neither entertainers nor instructors.
But to persuade, they told what they had
seen and felt. First came the experience—some
direct communication, as they understood it, from
Jahveh; then its description to the prophet's
audience.

For the most part, it would seem that these
experiences came detached, and, at least in time,
independent of one another. The actual prophetic
words, as we have them, generally group themselves
in short paragraphs or strophes. These strophes
are rhythmical or even in metre; the distinction
between rhythm and metre is not always easy to
draw, though the difference from the plain
narrative prose used elsewhere is clear at once.
The style varies as much as Wordsworth's *Laodamia*
varies from the *Lyrical Ballads*; but the language
is always tense, direct, imaginative, and emotional;
it is essentially poetical, and sometimes it reflects
a high degree of excitement.

At other times, the experiences described spring
from the prophet's reflection on his own life, his
purposes and their fulfilment, as notably with
Hosea's marriage, and Isaiah's two sons and their
names.[1] The absence of anything that might be
called definitely abnormal in these two prophets is
all the more striking when we turn to Ezekiel with
his descriptions of the weird and grotesque actions
he felt himself bidden to perform, his second sight,
and his half-mad sword-song. Evidently, the
actual reception of the message was known as a
definite and soul-stirring inspiration. Often, the

[1] Hosea i.; Isa. vii. 3, viii. 3.

excitement returns as it is being described. But what happened when it first came? Was the prophet right when he thought that some one else spoke to him? If so, who was this person? Was the prophet's Jahveh identical with our God, the Father of the Lord Jesus Christ? If we cannot answer this question, we can say very little to purpose about the prophets. We cannot however answer it at the present. Nor can we hope to answer it till we have studied the one prophet whom we know at all intimately, Jeremiah himself.

These prophets, however, are marked also by another characteristic. They are all of them, in the main, prophets of adversity and disaster. A century before Amos, Micaiah had to protest against the glib certainty of the official spokesmen. "Go up and prosper, for Jahveh hath delivered the city into thine hands." "If thou return at all in peace," Micaiah rejoined, "Jahveh hath not spoken by me." The words might be taken as a text for his successors. "Samaria will fall, and that soon," was the message of Amos and Hosea. Although Jerusalem was destined to survive Isaiah by more than a century, one would gather both from Isaiah and Micah that fate was on its way, as stern and as speedy. True, Hosea suggests repentance and forgiveness; and Isaiah foretells the striking deliverance of Jerusalem in 701 (unless this should be dated in 689), and the future coming of the Messianic age. But the general and unmistakable effect is one of gloom and disaster.

This was puzzling enough, as we can clearly see, to an audience which had learnt to think of Jahveh as a saviour and deliverer, from the days of the Red

Sea onwards, and whose eschatology rested on the ultimate triumph of Jahveh over all his own and his people's enemies. But the prophets, if they assumed disaster, did so as men who knew the character as well as the will of Jahveh. They were less interested in what he was going to do in the future than in what he was demanding in the present. Hence, the value and force of their moral and religious teaching. The Jahveh whom they served was a god who demanded honesty, kindliness, and humble reliance on himself, who could be deflected by no prayers and propitiated by no sacrifices; whose power was as supreme in the world of international politics as in the individual soul; whose mercy responded promptly to every movement of repentance or act of amendment; who was bound to his own chosen people as a husband to his wife; and who rewarded simple obedience and trust with complete security and peace. However discontinuous were the prophets' "auditions," voices heard on hillside or in street or temple as Joan heard hers in the fields and farmyard at Domremy, they shared one body of convictions, and when the voices spoke, to that body of convictions they were always true.

Such was the fellowship to which Jeremiah, as a "Nabi," knew himself to be called. Nor had he to wait long for his first voice. When it came, it was indeed significant. He was told to go and shout in the ears of Jerusalem the following words (ii. 2-4—McFadyen's version):

I remember the love of thy youth—
An affectionate bride wast thou—

When thou followedst me through the desert,
　A land that is all unsown ;
Then Israel belonged to Jahveh,
　His first fruits, sacred to him.
Whosoever devoured her was punished,
　On such did disaster fall.

He starts with the word " love " ; a word that
was constantly on the lips of Hosea, though unknown
to Amos and even Isaiah.　But there is a difference
in Jeremiah.　Hosea thinks chiefly of the love of
the husband for the unfaithful wife.　Jeremiah
thinks of the earlier years when bride and bridegroom were mutually devoted, years fated to be
clouded over but too soon, yet never forgotten.
Few modern readers can quite appreciate the daring
of this conception.　" If you want to think of God
aright, think of Him as a Father."　Such is the
message of the Gospels.　" If you want to think of
Him aright, think of Him as your husband, and
yourself as His bride."　Such is Jeremiah's conception.　What an intimacy of mutual dependence
it suggests between God and man.　On the other
hand, in the New Testament, the Father's child is
the individual.　In Jeremiah, the husband's bride
is the nation.　The individual Christian can say,
" I am my Father's child."　No individual Hebrew
could say, " I am Jahveh's bride."　There are
indeed plenty of indications that Jeremiah's contemporaries held a belief in the existence of a divine
consort for Jahveh, as for Baal ; a belief that could
not but be appallingly fruitful of evil practices.
Jeremiah's first word, if it is a proclamation, is also
a protest.　Jahveh has one consort, and this is—
Israel.　And Jahveh is not merely a god of law,

penning the Decalogue or thundering from Sinai.
His first thought is not even of obedience, but of
the answer which warm personal affection longs for
from its object. To the spirit of this word he
remained true all his life. Other prophets might
pass from one message to another. Jeremiah can
never be properly understood unless we remember
that whatever else he is saying, he is always saying
this.

This first word was quickly followed by others.
No indication is given us, until much later, of time,
date, or occasion. Sometimes the different paragraphs or stanzas that fill a chapter are clearly
connected in thought; sometimes they are as
clearly independent. Each passage must be judged
on its merits. It is never safe to conclude that
because two passages occur together in our present
collection of Jeremiah's writings, they must have
been delivered consecutively. We do not know on
what principle or principles Jeremiah's remains have
been strung together. The deciding factor in the
arrangement seems generally to have been some
real or fancied resemblance in the subject-matter
or even the language. We only know that the order
is not uniformly chronological; and there are
passages (some scholars would say many passages)
which cannot be considered to be by Jeremiah at
all.[1]

---

[1] For deciding these questions we can have only internal
evidence. But that evidence may be very strong indeed. For
example, in xvii. 19–28, we find a view of the Sabbath which is not
only absent from all the rest of the book, but which is in clear
contradiction to Jeremiah's conception of Jahveh's demands. If
Jeremiah had actually attached this importance to the Sabbath (an

In what follows this first word, however, we can detect without difficulty a single clear train of thought. It may be that the utterances are distinct. Many of them are introduced by the words " Thus hath Jahveh said," and they close with " Oracle of Jahveh." But one leads on to another as if a train already laid was being slowly fired. " Why, asks Jahveh, should you have left me ? What wrong have I done you ? Did I not bring you through the desert to the land where now you dwell ? " (ii. 5–7). Then a deeper note is struck. " Your renunciation of me is deliberate. You have turned from me to idols ; what a horrible thought. No other nation has ever done the like. So I cannot let you rest " (ii. 8–12). " Hence," he continues,

importance which, so far as we know, was only felt after the exile), he could hardly have refrained from referring to it in some other part of his work. Similarly, with the magnificent prophecy against Babylon (l. 1–li. 58). Jeremiah, as we shall see, never utters elsewhere a single word against Babylon, either by way of prediction or warning. As a matter of fact, all his later troubles were connected with his consistent refusal to do so. We should therefore have to suppose that at some period of his life he completely changed his mind, and that he had previously said what he was subsequently attacked for having refused to say. There is nothing to suggest such a change, nor any period of his life into which we could fit it. In some of the other prophecies against the nations (notably that against Moab, chap. xlviii.) there is much that we find elsewhere ; and little in any of them that is characteristic of Jeremiah, as we know him from the prophecies that we cannot doubt. We are, therefore, justified in leaving them out of our study. When the art of book-binding was still unknown, it was easy for detached and anonymous pieces of prophecy or poetry to be affixed to larger collections, and then to be thought to proceed from their authors. In this way many of the better known prophets gained credit for work with which they themselves had nothing to do.

"come your misfortunes and perplexities. How, indeed, could anything else result?" It is not a case of sin and punishment so much as of cause and effect. Then Jeremiah's mind turns to the licentious worship of the country shrines. "Sheer harlotry. An ineffaceable stain." "You have simply been giving yourselves up to your own lust, running the very shoes off your feet. But do not suppose that these gods of yours can save you when trouble comes." "To no purpose have I punished you. You have forgotten me sooner than a girl would forget her trinkets. You say, you are innocent; yet your guilt is patent; and ruin is inevitable" (ii. 29–37).

All this, be it noted, is directly attributed to Jahveh. The prophet does not say that he is uttering what he personally thinks about God, like a modern preacher. Jahveh actually *is* the outraged husband who is speaking. Israel's early romance has long since passed away; but Jahveh is still made to speak as a lover rather than a judge— a lover whose language is touched with vivid realism and embittered by despair; who sees and (such is the paradox of thwarted passion) dwells on the wantonness of the object of his love. He has no hope; and the misery of it is—"tu l'as voulu!"

As the young prophet brooded over his country's sin, its horror increased. Had Desdemona really been what Othello was led to imagine, we might compare Jeremiah's language in iii. 1–5 with Othello's terrible inability to keep the foulest words from his tongue. "Even if you wanted to come back now, how could I take you?" And then comes one of the surprises which meet us so often in Jeremiah (iii. 19–25 ; iv. 1–4). " How I would have welcomed you ; but you would not come. And yet—there are the sounds of weeping, the signs of penitence." " We have sinned, and from our sins we have gained nothing. We can but come back in our shame to thee." " Ah, if you will indeed return," is the reply, " you will be a blessing to the whole world. But you must break up all the untilled ground of your heart, and the circumcision, the sign of your devotion, must not be in your flesh, but in your soul."

Was Israel then doomed, or not ? Who could say ? Jeremiah could not. Looking at those centuries of faithlessness, what hope was there ? Yet, if once there came a cry of real repentance— a cry which Jeremiah seems to put on their lips— the arms would be open once more. The passionate exhortation is that of a youth too eager, and perhaps too inexperienced, for much detailed political knowledge. He is not like Amos, able to point to one event after another in the confused political world of his day. There are indeed references to coquetry with Egypt and Assyria, which doubtless Isaiah would have expressed in very different fashion ; but the calamities of which he speaks are quite unidentifiable ; the past, like the future, was but the background to the ever-present and unchanging sequence of sin and suffering. What Jeremiah knew (and this was of far more importance than a hundred historical details), was that if penitence was to avail, it must be what it had never been yet, the turning of the mind and will. Naturally the lover does not desire the mere gestures of affection : only affection itself can satisfy him.

These utterances were not confined to Anathoth. Indeed, since an hour's walk would bring the prophet from his home into the centre of the capital, it is easy to suppose that even if the limit of each prophecy were the brief stanza, he would go into the city to deliver it. But when he went there, he kept his eyes open. Perhaps, as a youth, he had expected a level of piety and receptiveness there, in the very courts of the temple, so to speak, which could not be found in his little country town. If so, he was bitterly disappointed. In a passage that reminds us (v. 1–14) of Socrates' account of his search for wisdom in Athens, or the story of Diogenes and his lantern, Jeremiah describes how he searched Jerusalem for an honest man. Even one (not simply ten, as when Abraham pleaded for Sodom) might have secured the city's pardon. But in vain. The great men were even worse than the poor. A city of law-breakers, of adulterers, who repudiated Jahveh, and could not escape. We have a second picture in v. 20–31 ; wealth, luxury, riot, callousness, oppression ; all duties forgotten, all laws defied. The prophets, inspired spokesmen of Jahveh, were themselves liars ; the priests, the regular ministrants of the shrine, guided their teaching by these lies ; and society was content. A further outburst (vi. 6–21) shows how deep is the effect of the city on him. He had tried to hold back the divine anger seething in his heart. He can do so no more. Covetousness and falsehood everywhere ; every warning despised, till at last foreign invasion would swoop on them, and what good would their sacrifices be to them then ?

It is clear that Jerusalem paid no attention at all to this young man from the country. Probably he was at once put down by most of those who listened to him as something of a madman. His interpretation of the history of the country must have seemed fantastic and absurd. What a wild view of the past, to call it all one long piece of unfaithfulness. A galling thing, indeed, for the young prophet to find his new and profound convictions neglected or laughed at. If they had gripped him less closely, he might have despaired. But this reception leads him to another discovery. His warnings are to serve a further purpose. They are to bring the hidden character of the nation to light, and show it for what it is. The prophet's duty is to test the " silver," and to pronounce it dross.[1] He must reveal Jahveh to man : he must reveal men to themselves (vi. 27–30).

This rejection was only what was after all to be expected. He had himself become assured, at the moment of his " call," that he would be in perpetual opposition. Or did he think that the " building up " would follow immediately on the " pulling down " ? And neither his message, nor its reception, was wholly unprecedented. He had had his predecessors. The path of Manasseh's reaction had been marked by the martyrdom of his opponents; and the protests of Zephaniah, for

[1] For " watch-tower," vi. 27, read " metal tester." Perhaps Jeremiah had learnt this duty from Isaiah (i. 25), but Jeremiah had none of Isaiah's hope. As so often, Ezekiel (xxii. 19) takes up Jeremiah's ideas.

anything that Jeremiah appeared to think, had ended in nothing. Zephaniah was related to the royal house of Judah ; and those who listened to him must have thought him more intelligible, and more important, than the youthful enthusiast from Anathoth. He gives us, indeed, a good deal more information about the state of things in Jerusalem. He describes the worship of the stars, both in the temple, and on the roofs of private houses, the continuation of the old Canaanite Baal cult along with the newer cult from Assyria, and the pagan custom of jumping or stepping high over the threshold that the Hebrews were imitating. He, too, speaks of searching the city in vain for an honest man, and he scourges the greed and violence of society. It was evidently a period of commercial activity and expansion ; but this, as always in Jerusalem, meant new wealth for the rich, new poverty for the poor. His own upper classes were as corrupt as the priests (he prefers to use a contemptuous term and calls them " shavelings ") and the prophets. The king himself he does not mention. The king was still young, and, at least in the early part of his reign, when Zephaniah was preaching, surrounded by men who, after the fall of Amon's murderers, carried on Amon's policy.

But there was more in Zephaniah's message than this. No one in Judah could be insensible to the events of the period in Western Asia. Josiah had been on the throne for little more than ten years before it was plain that the Scythians were once more on the move. No one could predict with any certainty what their attitude to the more settled countries would be at any given time; least of all whether they would choose to be the friends or foes of Assyria. It was now some fifty years since they had first appeared in Asia. Herodotus has a story that when Nineveh was besieged by Phraortes the Mede, the siege was raised by the Scythians, who thus gained possession of the whole of Asia, and held it for twenty-eight years. In any case, it seems clear that they were pressing on the north-west of the Assyrian empire as early as 678 B.C.[1] When it was known that they were pushing southwards, everyone would be asking " whither " ? Zephaniah, sharing the general excitement, describes a striking vision of their desolation of the Philistine coast-line. Naturally, they would take the coast-road rather than travel along the central mountain range. But they would not stop there. Zephaniah did not expect them to attack Judah; but he pictured them working round to Moab and Ammon, territories which were more exposed to a nomad horde, and then turning east and attacking Nineveh itself.[2]

This, as we shall see later, did not take place. The attack which they finally launched on Nineveh was made under very different circumstances. But Zephaniah was left with a deep sense of disappointment for another reason. He had hoped that the near approach of this terror would recall the people of Judah to their senses. It did not. If it failed, he asked, could any warning be effectual ? He could only expect what Isaiah had foretold long ago, that some terrible disaster would at last befall

[1] Herodotus, i. 103–106.   [2] Zeph. ii.

the little state, and that at best a small remnant
would escape.[1]

Jeremiah would naturally hear the utterances of
Zephaniah in Jerusalem. He would certainly be
aware of the excited rumours that filled the streets
and bazaars; and the thought of the terrible
Scythian advance acted on his already excited
mind like new wine. He now speaks again, as a
man thrown into a panic. But he does not speak
(and this is noteworthy) as a prophet. We possess
some six or eight brief but arresting poems—hardly
more than snatches of poetry—often referred to as
the "Scythian Songs," in which his emotions at
this time have found expression. And in them he
does not refer his words to Jahveh. He is for the
time the spectator of Jahveh's acts rather than the
mouthpiece of his word.

The first of these songs is a terrified warning to
the country people to collect behind the walls of
the cities. The "devastator of nations" (note the
vague weird language) has gone forth and Jahveh's
fierce wrath "rests upon all" (iv. 5-8). In the
next song (iv. 13-17) the approach of the foe is
described, in a passage reminding us of Micah i.,
and its whirlwind speed (very different, we may
suppose, from the more leisurely movements of the
heavy Assyrian infantry) from the extreme north
to the neighbourhood of Jerusalem itself—the dire
result of rebellion against Jahveh. With this must
be placed a poem which has been somehow dis-
placed (vi. 22-26) further describing the relentless
and disciplined advance of these riders from the
north, the dangers of the open country which they

[1] Zeph. iii. 12.

were now over-running, and all the sounds of mourning. To sounds, whether of joy or sorrow, Jeremiah was always peculiarly susceptible. We hear again the sinister word " devastator," and another, which will be repeated in very different circumstances, " terror on every side," *magor-missabib*, a long slow word with every vowel sounding like a knell.[1]

Next comes a cry of agony (iv. 18–22), in which sheer physical terror is joined to the misery of the thought that Judah has never suspected the real cause, her own sin. This is followed by the famous passage (iv. 23–26) in which Jeremiah, as if he were the last man left on earth, surveys a country from which all life has fled. The impression of utter desolation conveyed by these four strokes of the pen is marvellous. The passage has been claimed as a clear example of prophetic ecstasy. The first sense of horror may indeed have come on Jeremiah in an overwhelming rush. But the poem itself is no collection of random or ecstatic utterances. Its art is like that of the equally famous description of the drought in chapter xiv. : passing from the general gloom of emptiness in earth and sky to the shuddering of mountains and hills—not a man, not a bird, nor a cultivated field ; and every city in ruins, " laid waste by the fierce hot wrath of Jahveh." If, as Wordsworth held, it is the business of the poet to describe the experiences and emotions of a previous season of deep feeling, Jeremiah is certainly a poet here. He was as much, or as little, of an ecstatic as was Shelley when he wrote the *Ode to the West Wind*.

[1] *Cf.* p. 120.

E

So desolating a moment as this did not recur. But the terror remained. That Jahveh had ordained the calamity could not be doubted; and now Jeremiah sees the whole population taking to flight (iv. 27–31). He imagines the city trying to make terms—another harlot's trick!—and then struck to the ground, screaming like a woman in labour, beneath a murderer's dagger. The next song (vi. 1–5) is a parallel to this; but it is not now a matter of flight into Jerusalem, but out of it. The " laager " of these pastoral hordes is seen; and when they find that it is too late to take the city by day, they resolve to seize it with all the fury of a night attack.

Taken by themselves, these agonised outbursts throw a curiously mingled light on the mind of their author. He was evidently unmanned. We have already referred to Wordsworth. When England was in danger of invasion by a foe as relentless as the Scythians, Wordsworth blew from his clear trumpet strains as soul-stirring as those of his beloved Milton. Jeremiah's trumpet could only sound the signal for flight and despair.[1] " A mere poltroon," his hearers might have said. But Jeremiah was no coward, unless to be distrustful of oneself and to shrink from an all but impossible task is to be a coward. True, when we compare the effect produced on him by this expectation of

[1] Several of the expressions in the songs do not seem to fit the Scythians very well. This might suggest that Jeremiah was too disturbed to form any clear notion of what was frightening him. But, like many of his contemporaries, he had no personal knowledge of a Scythian invasion, and his imagination was therefore the more free. And it is probable that the poems underwent subsequent editing. See pp. 48 f.

the Scythians with that produced on Zephaniah, there is a difference. Jeremiah trembles as Zephaniah did not. That neither prophet counselled or thought of resistance is intelligible enough. The invasion was a scourge of God. As well blame Augustine for not laying down the pen which was writing the *De Civitate Dei* in order to recruit fresh legions for Rome. Zephaniah, however, could look on the future with calmness. Jeremiah could not. He expected the worst. And what the city was going to suffer, he would suffer ; what his countrymen would feel, he would feel ; and he did feel it. Here is the secret at once of his appeal, and of his isolation. He must denounce their vice, suffer their miseries, but never resist their foes. The foes were sent by Jahveh. He could do nothing but watch and tremble when they came. The heroic that was too high for others was his. He was denied the heroic that they could understand.

To crown all, the blow never fell. Zephaniah, indeed, had never said that it would, as far as Jerusalem was concerned. His own prediction about the Philistine coast was fulfilled. The Scythian hordes went on till they reached the borders of Egypt, and then Psamtik bought them off and sent them back.[1] But Jeremiah had described the wasting of Judah up to the very walls of Jerusalem, and then the fall of the city. The only thing that actually suffered was the reputation of

---

[1] Hdt. i. 105. Herodotus also mentions that on this " trek " they had the Medes with them. It is questionable, however, whether the Medes were at this time in a position to send an expedition so far afield, and whether they would have attacked the rival of their old enemy, Assyria.

the young prophet himself. No hint has reached us of Jeremiah's feelings when the Scythians left Judah untouched. To find that the horrible experience of the night was only a dream was indeed a relief; but to remember that he had assured every one that it was a prediction was to make himself a laughing-stock—perhaps to doubt his own sanity. Once listened to with rapt and horrified attention, now he only sees cold and incredulous eyes fixed on him. And the defiance, the infidelity of the city was as deep-seated as ever. There had been no reformation. Fear had not driven—it never can drive—to repentance. And now even the fear had passed. Had he then laboured in vain, and spent his strength for nought?

This was a question which he was to ask again. But to the attentive student this forecast of disaster from the Scythians was not quite as other predictions which seemed to miss their fulfilment. The excitement which led to the Scythian songs was psychic rather than religious. The omission of any reference to Jahveh's inspiration, noticed already, must not be put down to accident. For when the songs are examined carefully, they do not merely differ from the prophet's other work in the absence of the familiar phrases, "Thus hath Jahveh said," and the like. The whole tone is different. They are not in any sense homiletic or hortatory. They are imaginative and even frenzied descriptions of what Jeremiah thought was going to happen, and was even happening already. It is true that there are in the songs two references to the doom of Judah as fixed by Jahveh; in view of what he had said before, Jeremiah could hardly have been altogether silent on this. The fact that he is only just not silent is the more noteworthy. The songs were the product of a mood of morbid horror, induced by the passionate invectives which had preceded them, in a mind which had surrendered itself to brooding on the circumstances of a raid from the North. They were not the results of the deep moral conviction which he had already learnt to identify with Jahveh's voice.

But they reveal to us a good deal of the prophet himself. They were more than a cry of fear. We have seen that Jeremiah was not a coward. And they were no mere prediction of disaster, such as might have been uttered by Amos, or even, with his own stern detachment, by Isaiah. Jeremiah knew no detachment. A deep and burning sympathy sounds in them. He is terrified for his people. It is not a spectacle of vicarious suffering that he exhibits. The Jews must indeed drink the cup of Jahveh's wrath. But he, as one with them, will have to drink it too. He is the accuser of the people, the denouncer, the brazen wall and the fenced city. He stands also among the prisoners at the bar, the victims marked out for penalty. When we understand this, we begin to understand Jeremiah.

IV

A GREAT RELIGIOUS MOVEMENT
621–c. 616 B.C.

xi. 1–11 (p. 79); xxx. and xxxi. (pp. 81 *ff.*); xii. 1–4; xi. 18–23 (p. 84); viii. 4–13 (p. 86).

WHATEVER it meant for Jeremiah, the lifting of the cloud of Scythian invasion must have filled the statesmen in Jerusalem with immense relief. Uncertain as were their political sympathies, the Scythians had more than once given ground for the belief that they were the allies of Assyria, and the young king and his court had no wish to see any friends of Assyria within striking distance of Jerusalem. In spite of the gloomy prognostications of Jeremiah, Judah was not now, as Israel had been in the time of Hosea, ready to fall like a helpless prey into the hands of the minister of Jahveh's vengeance. The state was not even like the Israel that had listened to Amos' forebodings, when only folly could put far off the evil day. In spite of the Scythians, chastisement from the Assyrian empire, the rod in Jahveh's hand as Isaiah had called it, seemed farther off than ever. Assyria was now practically powerless. She had nothing to hope from her turbulent and capricious auxiliaries.

Egypt too showed small sign of movement or of interest in her old sphere of influence in Palestine. The little state of Judah could now enjoy a season of independence that her rulers had not known for over a century. It is true that for a really far-seeing statesman the sky was not unclouded. To a keen mind, the very cause of this growing freedom would have suggested apprehension. When the day of Assyria's fall arrived, what would happen in the scramble for her empire ? But there is little evidence of such long views among the statesmen of Western Asia. Josiah and his counsellors must have looked around them with increasing hopes. But Jeremiah would read in the brightening sky a doubt profounder than the doubt caused by the disappearance of the Scythians. Was evil to go unpunished ? Was crime to bring crime for ever ?

Meanwhile, the king began to prepare for the future which now rose before him. At some time since his accession, there had been what we should call a change in the government. The men who had surrounded his youth, and who had put down the conspiracy which had destroyed Amon, had fallen from power. Perhaps the now obvious weakness of Assyria was one of the causes of the change. But when we have any definite indication of Josiah's policy, we find it the opposite of Manasseh's. He and his leading statesmen now began to aim at complete independence. They set themselves to strengthen the capital as a political and an ecclesiastical centre, and to exalt the prestige of its worship. They could not hope to destroy the various local shrines scattered about the hills of Judah ; local ties and associations were, of course, far too strong. But the glories of the temple at Jerusalem—always, save at the worst times, true to the more puritan traditions of the imageless worship of Jahveh—could be renewed; and to exalt the temple, linked from its very dedication with the majesty of the house of David, was to exalt the position of the reigning monarch. Was it too much to hope that now at last, when there was no foreign power able to demand its tribute, impose its ritual, and quarter its officers in the capital, the tribes might assemble in the city of David even from the disorganised northern districts, and perhaps, fulfilling an ancient prophecy, the surrounding nations might join them on the sacred hill of Zion ? [1]

We must not smile at this naïve conception. Josiah was not the first to identify, quite honestly, true religion with the power and influence of the crown; nor was he the last. How could Jahveh be better pleased than by the honour of the building, and of the city, where he had set his name, and of the monarch whom he had anointed ? At all events, there was no one to dispute the point with him. The temple priests were naturally in agreement. Closely attached for centuries to the royal family to whom they owed their position, and quite willing to regard their temple, as Amaziah had regarded the temple at Bethel, as the "king's sanctuary," they had nothing to lose and everything to gain by steps which would bring an increasing number of worshippers to tread Jahveh's courts. They could have no fanatical desire for the restricted type of worship which rejected all cults save those which had their origin in the desert; and they might have felt no strong objection when Ahaz set up an altar of some Damascus pattern in

[1] Isa. ii. 2 *ff.*; Micah iv. 1 *ff.*

the temple courts, or Manasseh introduced the specific cults of Mesopotamia to please his Assyrian masters. But the worship of the country shrines was different. Its sensuous nature implied an appeal and an attractiveness which could not with any conscience be imitated in Solomon's temple in the capital; and the successors of Zadok could not be expected to feel kindly to the unofficial ministers of little townships which fondly clung to their local patriotisms and memories, and drew their inhabitants to altars so old that, in comparison, the temple was but of yesterday.

The prophetic guilds were as sympathetic to the court as was the priestly order. It is true that the prophets had no special interest in the temple; but they, too, were closely connected with the royal house; the glory of Jahveh as manifested in the national glories of Jahveh's people was their ideal; and they could not but welcome Josiah's determination to make Judah once more a power to be reckoned with. At the same time, they were regarded, and they regarded themselves, as in some sort the guardians of morality and good order. The greatest men who had borne the name of prophet had protested against the injustice and bullying that has always been the poison of public life in the East—the misuse of power, the seizure of land, the readiness to take bribes and to withhold wages—contraventions, one and all, of the sound old Hebrew traditions of democratic kindliness and honesty and good-will. Josiah believed in these traditions. He was in the best sense a conservative. All that was most genuine in the prophets recognised that his cause was theirs.

Josiah had another powerful support, on which he relied, possibly, more than on prophets or priests. He had with him a body of intelligent and high-minded statesmen, who understood him and sympathised with his ideals; perhaps it would be truer to say that they had taught him to sympathise with theirs. They were old enough to have known the darker days of Manasseh. Doubtless they were not unfamiliar with the arts well known to statesmen of the Tudor period in England, the *Realpolitik* which would build the throne on gold and iron. But, as they were to show more clearly later on, they stood by the older idea of the monarchy, and would have the king, in a phrase as well-known to Hebrew as to Western ears, the shepherd of the people.

To say that the king had now behind him a united nation might be too much. The wealthy merchants, the creditor class, and the owners of the larger estates were not likely to be on the side of a stricter morality; and the ideal of a purer worship had its enemies. But, at present, circumstances combined to keep these in the background, and Josiah could start without fear on his plan of concentration. It was to a certain extent a renewal of the policy of Hezekiah, and of the short-lived national confidence which was born of the retreat of Sennacherib. That crowning mercy, like Dunbar or the destruction of the Armada, could not be entirely obliterated from Jewish minds, and had been perpetuated in some glowing poetry. Isaiah's ringing defiance of the invader could wake a response in the hearts of every succeeding generation. Isaiah's was not the jingoistic nationalism of " my country, right or

wrong." His deep conviction had been that safety
was to come through "quietness and confidence";
that for Israel, as for Egypt (though in quite another
sense), strength lay in "sitting still," and that
armies were unnecessary allies for Jahveh of hosts.
Such teaching sounded as unintelligible in his days
as in our own. Nor had his hearers learnt even
from his lips the truth that only straightforward
dealing could keep a nation in its place, and that
Jahveh could be turned aside neither by prayers
nor sacrifices from the course on which he was set.
Still, there was a real desire for a higher standard
of conduct in public affairs and social relations;
nor could any priest who cared for the time-
honoured code of the "Book of the Covenant"
be unsympathetic to this aim. However they might
have disapproved Jeremiah's threats and denunciations, there must have been many people, in exalted
as well as in humble quarters, to whom his exhortations to the old morality had been by no
means unwelcome.

This plan involved the actual restoration of the
temple. Pious monarchs in Assyria and Babylon
often found it necessary to rebuild neglected
sanctuaries; and although we cannot suppose that
even in Manasseh's time the temple was neglected,
parts of it could easily drop out of repair. The
process was begun in 621 B.C., when Josiah had now
been king for nearly twenty years. And while the
work of restoration was going on, a startling discovery was made. In a forgotten corner of the
temple, or among the debris to be cleared out, was
found an ancient document, which, on examination,
proved to be a collection of legal enactments.

That such a volume should have been found was not in itself surprising. It appears to have been the custom, at least in Egypt, for important documents to be deposited in temples. The temples indeed were the safest places in antiquity, when there were neither repositories nor police forces. Thieves did at least "fear thunder"; and apart from various public archives, the priests appear to have been quite willing to receive more secular valuables into their custody. In fact, the temple often became a bank, and religion was thus the nurse of commerce as well as of medicine.

Still, even temples might fall into neglect, and the deposits be forgotten or lost. What was surprising about this document was its substance. The laws therein set down demanded something that no known document had ever hinted at, but that was in the main entirely in line with the official policy of the day. The only differences were that these laws went much further, and that they threatened the most serious penalties for disobedience. Not only was there to be one recognised centre of worship, but all other places of worship were to be destroyed. There was in it a great deal beside this; but this came at the beginning, and would naturally monopolise attention. It was at once brought to the notice of the head of the priests, Hilkiah; and as he read it, he must have seen the expression of something more than he had dared to dream of. If this were carried out, the centralisation for which they were working would be complete. He showed it to the chancellor Shaphan. Shaphan read it with his own eyes. Its importance was obvious. It must be presented without delay to the king. The effect on Josiah was identical. To destroy all the local shrines, to confine all worship to the royal sanctuary would have been too bold a step for most monarchs. Hezekiah had gained only a partial and temporary success in his attempt to carry out the plan. But with so authoritative a command behind him, Josiah might proceed where even Hezekiah had paused. One other step, however, was necessary before any decisive act of promulgation. Josiah must be sure that Jahveh was behind it, and meant it to be enforced. He therefore consulted a woman named Huldah, known to be possessed of prophetic or, as we might say, of oracular powers. The response was striking and full of encouragement, and it left no doubt that what-ever was enjoined, the penalties for disobedience were certain.

The way was now clear. Court officials, priests and prophets had accepted the new law and its divine sanctions. Opposition there might be ; but before such a combination opposition was of little account. The last remains of the traditions of Manasseh's reign could be swept away, and the possibility of any revival effectually removed. To our minds there is something a little unreal, or even perhaps ludicrous, in this sequel to an antiquarian discovery. Suppose, we ask, it had been a forgery ? Did not the idea strike Josiah's ministers ? It purported, as all Hebrew laws purported, to come from Moses. Why did they not attempt to verify this claim ? Their one reply would have been to say that this (as we should be bound to admit) was impossible ; but that they had obtained the highest

authority for the acceptance of it in the direct
message from Jahveh through Huldah. And it was
perhaps natural that they should not hesitate too
long over a plan of campaign which in itself was so
attractive to them. If Jahveh enforced it, to
trouble further about a Mosaic origin would never
have occurred to the Hebrew mind. The Hebrews
knew nothing about canons of criticism ; the book,
with Huldah's weighty support, was its own
authority. We may see in it a compendium of
the ideals of the more ardent spirits of Hezekiah's
time, lost perhaps in the stormy years that followed,
but written with stern faith and uncompromising
loyalty and principle ; not without tears and even
blood.

We, too, can read this book. It would appear to
be identical, in substance, with the central part of
the book of Deuteronomy.[1] And it may well be
that some of the noble preaching by which the legal
enactments are preceded and followed was actually
listened to by Josiah. The book opens with the
command to do away with all worship save at one
place—the place where Jahveh is pleased to put
his name ; and all through the book the haunting
words recur—a phrase so much more significant
than any mere place-name. Later on, the order
of the feasts and sacrifices is laid down—all familiar,
yet all rather more elaborate than the law that had

[1] This has been doubted by Hölscher because it is too vague
and idealistic, and by Dr A. C. Welch, because it is too concrete
and practical for such a reformation as was intended by Josiah,
or possible for his time. But the balance of probability is generally
held to remain with the view taken in the text. That the canonical
Deuteronomy contains many expansions and modifications in its
central chapters is possible and even probable.

been previously known ; this was the priests' section. Then there was a section dealing with government : the rules of succession, as we should call them ; the privileges of the crown ; the main lines to be pursued in foreign policy. This was for the king. Other kings might have hesitated. Manasseh would have made short work of the regulations. But there was nothing there which Josiah might not well accept and follow ; nothing that was not in harmony with the policy he was actually pursuing. And scattered up and down the book were various moral precepts ; exhortations to honesty and kindliness—laws we can hardly call them—which were to some extent familiar in the older code preserved for us in Exod. xxi.–xxiii. ; the duty of allowing the poor to glean after the harvest ; the duty of charity to the poor and unfortunate, and also (a significant addition) to the country priests, now to be dispossessed and (unless they cared to undertake subordinate duties in the temple) left to wander up and down the country-side like the helpless monks in England after the dissolution of the monasteries. All this would attract the better men in the prophetic class. There had always been a tradition of brotherly and sociable good-will in Hebrew life. The little communities of small farmers, all regarding them-selves as akin to one another, had fostered it ; and the more eminent of the prophets during the last hundred years and more, living at a time when changing conditions were threatening to sweep it away before a novel plutocracy, had vigorously championed and extended the simple old precepts, identifying them with the expressed and declared will of Jahveh, and exalting them above all the ritual and devotion of the sanctuary.

The authors of the book, indeed, did not, of course, go as far as the prophets. They did not hold that the worship of the altar was of no account at all. Very far from it. But they put conduct on the same level as ritual. For each they used a character word, *mishpat*, which has something of the double meaning of the Greek word νόμος, used both for custom and for law, but also going beyond it ; for it means also decision (the verb from which it comes=κρίνω, to decide a case) ; and all decisions are really from Jahveh. Thus the rules about conduct, enshrined in traditional morality, are as much the decisions of Jahveh as the rules for cultus, and can as little be disobeyed or neglected. And along with all this goes a relentlessness of penalty for the disobedient—there is no sacrifice for him ; only death—which would have satisfied Amos or Elijah. No wonder that Huldah was attracted and recognised the voice of Jahveh in the new law book.

What strikes us about the book, in fact, is its comprehensiveness. It is not a compromise ; it is a compilation, a general manual of national life, a corpus of instruction for all classes and conditions of men. It cannot indeed be called complete. It does not contain directions for all the cases where interests might clash and decisions be needed. What code could do this, even for the comparatively simple conditions of ancient Palestine ? Like the older " Book of the Covenant," [1] it is in large part a collection of precedents, to be followed in future

[1] Exod. xxi.–xxiii. 19.

disputes, like the *edictum perpetuum* of the Roman
prætors. But behind the precedents lie certain
broad and easily distinguished principles. It is a
brief conspectus of law and order and religion in
Israel, as conceived by the best minds in the nation.
The Book of the Covenant is different. It is
content for the most part to collect leading cases
in the life of a village community. Deuteronomy
pictures a whole nation at work.

There is another novelty in Deuteronomy ; the
emphasis on love. Love is the mainspring of
Jahveh's conduct to Israel, and of the response of
Israel to Jahveh. Conduct is important, but not
for its own sake. It is the manifestation or em-
bodiment of an attitude, which matters far more
than conduct itself. There is no precedent for
this in the older code. And it breathes a warmth,
a full-blooded humanity, so to speak, into the
catalogue of duties, which impresses every reader,
and which, six centuries later, was to attract an
eager and fearless youth in Nazareth. This note
was not indeed wholly new. It had been heard
more than a century ago in Hosea. Deuteronomy,
however, is not a mere echo of Hosea. It has none
of Hosea's attempt to picture the actual feeling of
Jahveh as a passionate tenderness, or to demand,
with an almost despairing insistence, the same
tenderness from Jahveh's " bride," the nation.
And Deuteronomy contains none of Hosea's lyrical
abandon. But no one who has caught the dis-
tinctive music of Hosea—silent in Amos, Isaiah,
and Micah—can miss it in the more precise and
measured yet still unmistakably fervent devotion of
Deuteronomy.

F

Such was the new instrument or Covenant of national order. "Covenant" indeed is a better term for it than "law." The word came easily to the lips of the Hebrews. A covenant or agreement between individuals naturally preceded anything like widely recognised and enforceable law in the history of society. And in those earlier days, when the modern sanctions of law-court, police and statutory imprisonment were unknown, an agreement becomes a religious proceeding and rests upon the sanctions of religion. Ordinary morality might differ from the precedents that governed the settling of disputes. Public opinion would gradually grow strong enough to enforce these, and agreements, too, would become increasingly matters of civil law rather than of religion. The Hebrews, on the other hand, had for centuries learnt to bring their morality and their civil law, like their cultus, under religious sanctions. In other words, law had to be obeyed because it was, what an agreement between individuals became, under the protection of the god. There was, however, this obvious difference. The god would enforce the observance of the agreement between the two human parties to it. But he was himself a party to the keeping of law. He laid down the terms ; and bound both himself and the other party, the nation, to abide by it. When, therefore, he is thought of as pre-eminently gracious and loving, the covenant or agreement is one of blessing, and any infraction of it by the nation is at once sin and folly.

Now in Deuteronomy this is precisely how Jahveh is conceived ; and, therefore, the upshot of the discovery of 621 was not the passing of an Act of Parliament or the promulgation of a new constitution, like a Bill of Rights or a Declaration of Independence; it was a spiritual transaction, a personal act of the whole nation. And although, like the framers of a marriage contract, Josiah and his people knew that very practical penalties would follow its infringement (the book itself made that quite clear), they were thinking, as one thinks at a wedding, of the vow and bargain itself.

The bargain once made, it was forthwith put into operation. For a parallel, we are led once more to the dissolution of the monasteries. Whether Josiah's commissioners were as thorough as those of Henry VIII., it is impossible to say. They probably met with more opposition. For in 1538 men had grown weary of the monks and their scandals, and they did not envisage the economic results of the king's drastic action. But even in England, when the monasteries had disappeared, no royal edict could entirely suppress all the worship of the old faith. Even if Josiah was as successful as he wished to be, and as the narrative in 2 Kings xxiii. implies he was, the inevitable opposition simply bided its time and waited for its chance to restore the old regime. The scandals of the local shrines might be as glaring as those of the monasteries and convents ; but there was no general moral revolt against them, unless the prophets, and Jeremiah among them, have been guilty of gross exaggeration in their invectives. In any case, the official iconoclasts (for such they must have seemed) were seen in every Judean town, as the sacred poles were cut down, the standing-stones flung to the ground, the venerated and often (to more puritan eyes) obscene objects of traditional worship broken and crushed, and, like churches used as barns, the ancient shrines were defaced and defiled. Such were the steps by which the temple in the capital was to become the one house of prayer for the whole nation.

And what did Jeremiah think of it all? We cannot tell. He has left no record of his thoughts at this time that can be identified. What would we not give for a letter or a speech dating certainly from 621! Yet it is not difficult to imagine what would be in the mind of an eager, impressionable, and mobile youth like Jeremiah in those momentous days. And we are not without some positive indications to assist us. His first prophetic impulse had spent itself. His attacks on the established worship had failed. Moreover, the predictions of the Scythian invasion had come to nothing. No one seemed a penny the worse, or the better, for either. "They call the prophet a madman," the youth must have said to himself bitterly. "They will certainly give that title to me." What wonder if he began to look back to the experience of five years ago and ask if its message was indeed genuine. He had no doubt indeed that Jahveh had spoken to him. He was never in doubt as to this. But had Jahveh told him the truth? Even though he refused this dreadful alternative, he had no message now, and no audience. The very necessity of silence, indeed, brought relief. To some men, five years of denunciation might have deepened resolve and hardened sympathy into defiance. Jeremiah was made of more sensitive stuff. A nature like his, calling out for friendship and gaiety,

the marriage song and the village dance, if faced
by the alternative of seclusion or opposition, would
naturally choose the former.

Then came the great discovery, and every serious
man in the country was stirred. Everyone who was
not thrown into hostility at once, found something
that carried further his own hopes or plans ; and,
intent on this, as generally happens, he neglected
the rest. But Jeremiah would notice what most of
the rest passed over. Here was a book that spoke
from first to last of love. It was not perhaps quite
the message of his own Hosea, or the text of his own
first sermon. On the other hand, there was no
mysterious deity surrounded by a wall of taboos, as
the priests had so often taught, but the voice of
affection and jealousy. Even the wild utterances of
wrath sprang from Jahveh's desire for his people's
loyalty. What a vindication of his earlier message !
Moreover, the book breathed the very morality of
the prophetic tradition. Honesty, kindliness, fore-
thought for the widow and the orphan, condemnation of the corrupt judge, patience with the debtor,
promptness in the payment of wages, sympathy
even with the young recruit in the army—all this
was of the very essence of the instruction of Jahveh
as he understood it. Such was the homely yet
noble type of conduct whose neglect would bring
ruin on the whole nation. What else had he himself
been saying ? And now this book of Jahveh's law,
guaranteed by a prophetess, was foretelling all that
he had foretold, but in yet darker images and with
more terrible threats.

No wonder he welcomed the book ; nor would it
be strange if he read more into its teaching than was

really there, and forgot certain sections (prominent enough to other readers) with which he could have little sympathy. His old message was given back to him, but with a double authority. First, it was an authoritative document, approved by Huldah as Jahveh's own word through Moses.[1] Second, all the prestige of the court and the government was behind it. It was as if (to take a modern parallel) an advanced and unpopular social reformer had found his most cherished projects embodied in a King's Speech. Two other points could not fail to attract him. This whole body of newly dis-covered law, like all that was best in what was more familiar, was a "covenant," a personal compact resting on good-will and loyalty. That was essential where Jahveh and Israel were concerned. And, noble as was the expression of the law, it purported to have been given to Israel at the end of the forty years in the wilderness, and it left un-challenged and untouched the majesty of those monumental ten words on Horeb which for ever bound together reverence to God and morality to men.

When, therefore, the covenant had been formally accepted and was to be carried out through the country, Jeremiah was ready for an unaccustomed but a very welcome rôle. It came, as did his earlier

---

[1] It is noteworthy that Huldah is not made to guarantee the Mosaic character of the book in 2 Kings xxii. 15 *ff*. She simply claims Jahveh's authority for saying that the penalties described in the book will come about, but that Josiah himself will die in peace. She does not even refer, like Josiah himself, in verse 13, to the sins of previous generations. Her reply certainly has the appear-ance of genuineness. But it would be as naturally understood to give the guarantee of which it said nothing.

activities, from what he felt as a direct command from Jahveh. He was to urge the covenant upon the people, reminding them of the original commands in the desert, and going back, as the law book itself went back, from the legislation in Moab to the thunders from Horeb or Sinai (xi. 4) ; and reminding them also of the continuous witness to the law throughout Israel's whole history in Canaan, a history not only of prosperity in the land flowing with milk and honey, but of disasters that recalled the disasters described so vividly in the speeches in Moab. One can hear the very phrases of Deuteronomy in his account of this summons to preach (xi. 1–11).

At first, all seemed to go well. Every class and section in the community apparently followed the king ; and when the commissioners proceeded to enforce the provisions of the new law in the towns round Jerusalem, there is no hint of serious opposition. To a man of Jeremiah's temperament, deeply suspicious of all worship which could fix the mind on externals, and detesting the ritual that went hand in hand with greed and even with lust, the desecration of the shrines was more welcome than the stabling of troopers' horses in a cathedral to a Roundhead colonel. It is not difficult to imagine him accompanying the officers and reminding the impressed and rather frightened spectators of the real demands of the law, not ritual at all, but moral. They listened now, as he had never seen his audiences listening before.

So much for Judah. But the prophet's gaze had never been confined to Judah. Like his own home at Anathoth, his mind was really turned northwards.

Josiah was busy enforcing the law in the country which had once been part of the Northern Kingdom. The returning loyalty of Judah would surely mean a return of another kind for Ephraim. Jahveh's purpose would be only half performed if Ephraim were still in exile. And was there not every reason to hope for a return ? Assyria was clearly breaking up. Her ancient victims would be able to shake themselves free. Might not the repentance of Judah be followed by the repentance of Israel ? And then what would prevent the restoration of the kingdom which for so long had ceased to exist ? [1]

We can almost watch the conviction taking shape. And the result is one of the most beautiful poems in the whole of Hebrew prophecy, and, one might almost say, a poem worthy to rank among the world's noblest lyrics. It is found at present contained in chaps. xxx. and xxxi. ; and though there are certain later additions, these can be removed without much difficulty, and we can arrive at the original poem with a good deal of confidence. As before, the inspiration, and the words, are attributed to Jahveh ; but the warm and glow-

[1] It is usual to suppose that the fall of Samaria meant the deportation of at least the greater portion of the inhabitants of Northern Israel. But a thought of the vast movement which this would imply, as well as the numbers involved in the later deportations from Jerusalem, shows that actual exile must have been the lot of the minority of the whole population. We know indeed from the treatment of the Armenians by the Turks, that deportation is very far from impossible ; and deported exiles might return. But what is chiefly in the prophet's mind is a spiritual return to allegiance to Jahveh, even where the language implies, like that of Second Isaiah, an actual journey across the desert.

ing affection of the prophet is visible in every line.

Like other poems, it is composed in stanzas, between which at first we cannot always see the connection. And it was natural for later readers, desiring to see the bearing of the poem on their own time, to make additions or annotations to the original words. This has led many commentators to split up the chapters into distinct compositions, or to date them, or large parts of them, in a much later period. (See Appendix II., p. 214.) But there is no real difficulty in reading the chapters as a continuous whole ; and a single *leitmotiv*, as P. Volz has called it, is heard from beginning to end, the reiterated " return."

The poem begins with a picture of distress and agony, as if the worst darkness were preceding the dawn (xxx. 5, 6), followed by a clear promise of redemption (vv. 10, 11). For a moment, Jahveh pauses, as if to hear the cries which were now so soon to end, and to remind the sufferers of their unfaithfulness (12–15) ; and then comes the picture of restoration : the cities are to be rebuilt on the site of their own ruins ; and the community is to endure from generation to generation in prosperity and joy (18–20). But such a scene, once envisaged, grows in distinctness and detail. The poet is in the desert, where Jahveh meets Israel, and we hear the mutual words of greeting, promise, and hope (xxxi. 2–5). This passes into the picture of the actual return. The cry " Jahveh hath saved his people " rings out in the mountains, and we see the host of returning exiles, stumbling out of the mists of the north, finding their road made easy as they come, till when they reach sight of home their joy breaks into rapturous singing (vv. 6–14).

But this is not all. A second stanza is more sombre, as well as more dramatic, and nearer to actual possibilities. For the prospects of return seemed still far off. And how could a man of Jeremiah's deep ethical convictions contemplate such a return unless accompanied by an obedience hitherto sadly lacking ? Some forty years later, Ezekiel was to provide another answer to the question. He believed that when the nation had been restored, and found itself in undeserved prosperity, its conscience would be awakened, and it would begin to loathe itself for the sins of the past. Jeremiah, however, does not conceive that penitence will be so long delayed. He hears across the hills the voice of the ancient tribal mother Rachel, buried at Ramah, lamenting from her tomb her absent children. But she is comforted by Jahveh himself. And then the prophet hears a second voice. Rachel's children, in their distant exile, lament not only their sorrow but their sin. The sorrow at last is seen as chastening, and the sin is felt as shame. Immediately comes the joyous response from Jahveh. The divine pity can now have free course. " Set up the sign-posts along the homeward road, and let the virgin of Israel return." An unheard-of marvel ; but it is Jahveh's doing (vv. 15–22).

The stanzas are tantalisingly brief ; but they were remembered and pondered over. And they inspired two of the most touching poems in the subsequent literature, Ezekiel's picture of return,

already mentioned, and the restoration songs of
Second Isaiah. Jeremiah's poetry has a tense
energy which we miss even in the greatest of his
imitators. But his note was soon destined to
change. The reforms, which had started with
such promise, involved two consequences, which a
shrewd statesmen might have foreseen, but which
would hardly occur to the idealist hopes of the poet.
The first was that popular opposition soon began to
manifest itself. The religious associations of generations were being destroyed. Local feeling was
outraged. The old jealousy of the country towards
the capital was roused. After all, Jahveh had been
worshipped at these shrines and high places long
before the temple at Jerusalem had been thought of,
in the old days, when Jerusalem was still the last
stronghold of the heathen Jebusites. What right,
men would ask, had these ecclesiastical officials from
the city to come and tell them that all their traditional loyalties were a sin, and that their communion
with Jahveh beside their beloved altars was a
delusion ? How did Huldah or anyone else know
that Jahveh meant them to have no means of
approaching him save by a long journey to the
capital ?

So they may well have argued. If there was no
widespread religious movement, as in our own Reformation, neither was there a deep sense of political
and economic injustice, as in France in 1789. A
certain amount of political feeling, indeed, would
point in the opposite direction. The party of
Manasseh was not dead, and the peasants in the
country had little to hope from the preponderance
in the state of the magnates in Jerusalem. They

were no longer afraid of Assyrian armies trampling over their fields. Why could they not be left to themselves ? The upshot of it all was that the reforms had really little effect outside the city itself. The commissions might come, but they would go ; and the old regime would continue. Even Anathoth, almost within a bow-shot of the walls of the city, felt itself in this matter to belong to the country. And the family of Abiathar, with its lands, its memories, and its local influence, would certainly not make the way easier for the aims of that Zadokite priesthood which ever since Solomon's time had supplanted it in Jerusalem.

How could the indignation gathering there vent itself more naturally than on Jeremiah ? Jeremiah could not but perceive this ; and he was again plunged into doubt and misgiving (xii. 1–4). Jahveh could not be false. Yet among men, falsehood alone seemed to prosper. The popular acceptance of the covenant was a mere piece of outward conformity. "Drag them out," he prayed in a burst of anger, "like a flock of sheep destined for slaughter." The outburst was followed by a quick intuition, interpreted, like many others that were to come later, as direct information from Jahveh. Things were even worse than he had suspected. It was not merely dogged opposition that he had to meet ; but a plot against himself, from his own family (xi. 18–23). It was the fact ; and he had the clue. Behind the dark and menacing glances and the sullen silence which had been meeting his frank affection and confident hope, lay a conspiracy to make him, their kinsman, like the sheep doomed to the knife. So deeply implanted was their real hostility to the reformation, and to him, its prophet. The revulsion of feeling was speedy. A second burst of indignation called on Jahveh to avenge him on them ; and his anger told him that the prayer would speedily be answered. But the clouds had gathered again. He must leave Anathoth. Once more he was alone.

The two passages just considered remind us of the narrative of the prophet's call. We meet once more the two voices. And we shall meet them again. Ever since his call, save in the Scythian songs, we have heard but one ; every word that has been recovered is set down more or less explicitly as Jahveh's. Now we are aware again of expostulation and reply. Nor can we be satisfied to say merely that the prophet was debating with himself. The distinction between the voices is too clear. Jeremiah is impulsive, passionate, moving at a bound from self-pity to indignation, from indignation to vindictiveness, from vindictiveness to intercession. He exhibits that curious mingling of harshness and resignation which we see in the stories about Moses, and sometimes detect in the Apostle Paul. Now he will pray for his enemies ; now he will call down fire on their heads. Jahveh, on the other hand in these colloquies is stern, unbending, " jealous," swayed neither by curses or pleadings, but determined to give the prophet no respite in his task of denunciation. Shrinking from the task or even rebellious, Jeremiah can no more escape than Kundry could escape from the power of Klingsor.

But we must now pass to the second consequence of the reform, which was still more significant.

Even where the king's writ could run, the results
were not what Jeremiah had expected. Perhaps,
indeed, they disappointed the king himself. For
even in Jerusalem it soon became clear that while
the ritual element in the new code was stressed,
the moral was forgotten. The reformation was to
be a reform of cultus, but not of conduct. Now,
a change in conduct was all that Jeremiah really
cared about, and all, as he felt, that Jahveh really
cared about. But he cared so much for this change
in conduct, enforced as it was in the new law
book, that for its sake he could, at the moment,
altogether overlook the emphasis laid in that
book on ritual. Here he was entirely in line with
the great prophets who had preceded him. But
for conduct the priests, in the main, cared nothing.
So long as they could bring the worshippers from
the villages to the city, they were satisfied. The
great religious movement, welcomed with such
high hopes, was a failure. It was no true covenant between God and man. It left the heart
untouched.

   This, then, he said to himself, was the end for
which he had been working. Was such a law as
the priests were enforcing worth fighting for at
all ? It was worse. As they were interpreting it,
it was a piece of merely ritual legislation. As such, it
was a fraud, an imposition, a lie (viii. 4–13). Jahveh
could never have commanded such a " reform "
as this. It was a backward step. The state of
morals was worse rather than better. The very
instincts of the homing bird might have led them
to Jahveh ; instead, they rushed into evil with a
kind of wild fury. The guardians of this new law

had turned it into a forgery. The leaders of the reform, in shameless wickedness, were simply deluding the state into a deeper ruin, lulling the fears that might have meant caution and safety until at the last the fig-tree would be left with not a leaf that was not withered.[1]

---

[1] It has often been held that Jeremiah welcomed the reformation of 621, preached for it at first (xi. 1 ff.), and then remained silent during the rest of Josiah's reign. Others urge that viii. 4–13 shows that he opposed it from the first. This, as we have seen on pp. 77 ff., is probably not the case; but if, as is argued in Chap. V., the "colloquies" (xviii. 18–23, etc.) cannot be placed at a period after Josiah's death, the disillusionment must have come comparatively early, and this is what we should expect from the mingled effect that the law book would naturally have on such a character as Jeremiah's.

V

REACTION

c. 616–608 B.C.

xxxi. 31–34 (p. 89); xviii. 18–23 (p. 92); xvi. 1–9 (p. 93);
xx. 14–18; xx. 7–12; xvii. 9, 10, 14–18 (pp. 95 *ff.*); xv. 10–21
(p. 97); xiv. 1–16 (p. 101); x. 19–22 (p. 102).

SUCH was the end of Jeremiah's hopes from the
reformation. The brief period of expectation had
been followed by this utter disappointment. Yet
he could not surrender all the prospect, or believe
that though this agreement was no better than a
forgery, there was to be no new covenant at all.
As it stood, the law book was turning out to be
only a snare. It was full of provisions which were
worthless, and it was written down on parchment
or stone. How different from that other covenant,
the ten words, which were given on Horeb when
Israel was first brought out of Egypt, in those
happy days of early unstained love. Those words
contained nothing that could be twisted by priests
to the prestige of their order or the pomp of a
dishonest ritual. If Jahveh had ever given commands to his people, they were engraved there.
And they came from one Jahveh—not a multitude
of Jahvehs, each at his own shrine; and not to be
worshipped with any image or carved stones. All
that was valuable in Josiah's book was already in
those ten words; no theft, no murder, no adultery,

no perjury—all the cardinal sins of the prophet's days were forbidden there. What more could be needed? If these were obeyed, the golden age would return. But could any sane man look for obedience, with the record of the past before him? The whole nation was corrupt, diseased, and all that the priests could do was to cover up the symptoms, and pretend that concealment was cure. The covenant was broken, as men might break the stones on which it was inscribed. A new covenant was needed. And for Jeremiah to see the need was to be sure of its ultimate fulfilment; so sure of it that he could announce it. Inscribed stones were no good. All the past was the proof of that. The great words must be written on men's brains. When the Hebrew said "heart," he did not think of the emotions, but of the thought, the purpose, the will, the whole mind of the man. There, at the centre of his own personal life, the covenant was to be enshrined. There would then be no more need of instruction; no priests to give their authoritative Torah to ignorant and easily misguided men. Each man would be his own authority, for each would be in close and personal touch with Jahveh himself. Then, and not till then, would sin be a thing of the past (xxxi. 31–34).

It was a bold, and indeed an epoch-making anticipation; so bold that some (needlessly, as we may think) have doubted whether it could have come to Jeremiah at all.[1] It contained within itself the denial not only of the authority of the written word, but of the whole traditional view of Jahveh's

[1] See Appendix I.

relation to the nation.   If Jahveh were to write his
ten words on the heart, he would have to deal with
individuals.   Such a dealing with individuals had
never been made explicit before, or even, by most
people, thought of as a possibility.   Yet it is not
difficult to see how Jeremiah was driven to it.
With him, up to this time, as with every Hebrew,
the covenant was a fixed idea.   Jahveh dealt with
his people by a solemn agreement.   And that he
would finally reject his people, Jeremiah could not
as yet believe.   In moments of terror or indignation he might think of it.   He might announce
some dreadful calamity.   He did not believe that
Israel would be entirely cast off.   Other prophets
had expected that somehow the nation, or a part
of it, would survive.   But Jeremiah could not be
content with any sort of eschatological vagueness.
If the covenant of stone was useless, some other
covenant would have to be provided.   Where
could it be written, save in the heart of man ?
Probably Jeremiah did not understand all that his
words implied.   Ezekiel certainly did not understand his own much more thorough-going individual-
ism (chaps. xviii., xxxiii.).   But curiously enough the
idea of individual responsibility had been antici-
pated in Josiah's law book itself.[1]   For it contained
a provision that no one was to be punished for the
sins of his family (a condemnation of the whole
system of blood revenge, which was not the least
daring of its innovations).   Jeremiah himself must
have been struck by this provision, for, in a passage
prefixed by later editors to his announcement of
the new covenant,[2] he referred to it, perhaps un-

[1] Deut. xxiv. 16.   [2] xxxi. 29 f.

consciously, when discussing the familiar difficulty of the children who suffer for the parents' sin.

We may feel, indeed, that Jeremiah went much further than Deuteronomy. A law written on the heart marks the whole transition from outward conformity to inward acceptance. It means that delight in the law after the inward man on which Paul writes with such enthusiasm. It means that in Paul's sense the law, that is, the law " written in ordinances, touch not, taste not," and so on, is abolished six centuries before Paul. Jeremiah points to a time when men would not be under the law, but under grace.

But it often happens that a man misses the full point of the words he uses. Certainly Jeremiah was not ready—he never grew ready—to give up the idea of the corporate guilt of his nation, simply because he had learnt that the impulse to obedience must be individual. And, however noble the words sound to us, with all the majesty of the associations of Pentecost shining round them, we cannot forget that the covenant is not the last word to describe God's approach to men. Hosea might have taught Jeremiah that truth; indeed, he might have learnt it from his own earlier words. And it would seem that in the near future he was going to learn it in another and more tragic fashion. The words which express a great truth may flash upon the mind in an illuminated instant; to understand the inner meaning is the work of sorrow, prolonged strain, agony; and that was to be the experience of Jeremiah.

For he was now, after this, recognised as a dangerous man. He had not only alienated the priests, but the statesmen and the prophets as well. He had dared to oppose the policy which still united every party and section in the capital. Such conduct could naturally not be allowed. It amounted in their minds to claiming the support of Jahveh for what was sheer irreligion. He was defying all the leaders of the community. They set themselves, like the enemies of a yet nobler foe in the same city, to find material in his speeches for a capital charge (xviii. 18–23). The plot was laid; but, like the former plots, it somehow went wrong. There were influential men in the city, as we shall see later, who were unwilling to surrender Jeremiah to his enemies. We do not know their reasons for this. There may have been some family connexion. Or we might compare Paul's friendship with the Asiarchs at Ephesus. A man who showed, as Jeremiah did, recognisable signs of inspiration, would certainly command a good deal of popular respect; and, with the knowledge of intrigue around him, he may have taken care not to place himself in the intriguers' power. But the knowledge of the plot stung him, as he had been stung before. He has left on record a bitter cry for vengeance. He had pleaded for them once, he says; this was their return. Let them be abandoned to famine and sword; let their guilt never be pardoned and their sin never be blotted out!

We may lament such words. We shall never understand Jeremiah if we do not ponder them. Such fierce resentment, in a nature that is not ignoble, is only born of disappointment and disillusion. It is the language of rejected affection;

of desire for warm human companionship confronted by the certainty of perpetual loneliness. Such disappointment might leave others dumb. It provoked in natures like Jeremiah's a violent re-action, short-lived perhaps, but bitter and poignant. He had faced the disappointment, in a sense, ten years ago, at his call. Yet he had hoped, as a man will, against hope. Now there was no escape. For indeed at this time, if not before (it could not well have been later),[1] he knew that he was to be a celibate (xvi. 1–9). How could he marry and bring up children, when dreadful forms of death were to come on the whole nation ? Like every Hebrew youth (and he was more than a youth now) he had looked forward to marriage and " the voice of mirth and gladness, the voice of the bridegroom and the bride," the happy voices to which, with aching heart, he refers so often; but all such music was to sink into silence, and for him, who with his warm affectionate nature had longed for it as much as any man, it was never to come to utterance. Hosea's wife had left him for other men ; Ezekiel's wife was taken from him after years of marriage. Had Jeremiah to tear from his heart some face that he had longed to keep there for ever ?

He was now flung back on himself. One whole side of his nature was to be repressed. For some, this might have meant despair ; for others, what our psychologists call a neurosis. Jeremiah, too, is to exhibit moods which we can hardly help calling neurotic. Yet, as we examine the unique series of confessions in which these moods are

[1] See Chap. II., p. 28.

revealed, we can see much more than psychic instability. That, indeed, is not absent, but through it he comes to islands of certainty and insight which could hardly be reached save across these stormy seas. No other prophet has let in such a light upon his inner experiences. We catch a glimpse, indeed, of similar doubts and questionings with Habakkuk; and in one of the "Servant Songs" embedded in the second half of Isaiah, we overhear a note of perplexity and complaint, quickly suppressed.[1] But Jeremiah has left us some pages which remind the reader of parts of *Marcus Aurelius ad se ipsum*, though they are fired with a passion quite foreign to the wistful Stoic. Jeremiah, however, does not hold colloquies with himself. He pours out his soul to Jahveh; and Jahveh replies. The voice which Jeremiah knows as his own is one, Jahveh's voice is another.

We have no means of telling at what period or periods he passed through these experiences. They have been very variously dated, but generally in the strenuous days of Jehoiakim and Zedekiah, when the toils were already closing round the doomed city. But if we think of the prophet's psychological development, we shall be inclined to place them together, and in the period we are now considering. They are closely connected in tone. Jeremiah is continually wrestling with the same thoughts, and the vacillation he betrays fits but poorly with the more robust and confident defiance which, save for brief moments, he exhibits after 608. It would seem that after the shock of his

[1] Isa. xlix. 4.

disappointment over the reforms of 621, he passed
through a time of deep mental conflict, a sort of
" everlasting No." It was sharpened by the plots
of which he was the object ; and only towards the
end of Josiah's reign did he emerge, fortified by a
second " call," conscious of all that its new demand
for renunciation entailed, and ready for the still
sterner conflicts of his later years.

It is even more difficult to decide the order of
the passages we have now to consider. We cannot
be sure that the order in which they occur in the
" collected works " has any authority. The actual
order is perhaps unimportant. In conflicts of this
nature, territory has to be fought over again and
again. We " lose to-morrow the ground won
to-day." It is only after the lapse of time that we
can see where we failed, and

> " Not till the hours of light return,
> All we have built do we discern."

The order which is here suggested may be defended
as the order of thought ; and that is as much as
can be said.[1]

The series begins with a cry of despair, echoed
two centuries later by the author of the book of
Job. " Why was I ever born ? Curses on the day
which announced my birth. My whole life is one
long failure and shame " (xx. 14–18). Worse than
that. He had been seduced by Jahveh. The grim
possibility had occurred to him before, when his
anticipations of the Scythian invasion had been
falsified. But how much more ground was there
for it now ! The word he uses shows the bitterness

[1] *Cf.* the treatment in Skinner, *Prophecy and Religion*, chap. xi.

of his spirit. Hosea uses it of the lascivious tempta-
tions (too readily listened to) of Israel's lovers, and,
by a bold stroke, of Jahveh himself, taking their
place to " seduce " his beloved into the desert
where he was to regain her affection. And now
Jahveh is guilty of another kind of seduction,
alluring Jeremiah to the task which was to break
and crush him. The promises that came to him
at his call were sheer lies ; all that they had led to
was derision and contempt. Though he could not
shake Jahveh's message from him, it made him the
object of constant conspiracies and denunications.
" Yet "—in a sudden change of mood—" Jahveh
is with me ; it is my persecutors that shall stumble.
Cut them down, and let me see thy vengeance
upon them ! " So he appeals, as Job was to appeal
afterwards, from the Jahveh without, the Jahveh of
circumstances and appearance, to the Jahveh within,
who could not be false to his word (xx. 7–12).[1]

Next comes a curious passage, which shows with
pathetic clearness how the prophet is struggling to
firmer ground. " How can I know my own
heart ? All I know is that it is hopelessly sick."
Then it is that, for the first time, the other
voice is heard : " It is for me to know the heart. I
will see that each has his just reward." " Then
do thou, Jahveh, heal me. They mock at every
word of mine. They laugh at my predictions of
coming evil. As if I had desired the evil I foretold !
Let me know I have a refuge in thee ; and on them "
—another untamed outburst—" be confusion and
ruin ! " (xvii. 9, 10, 14–18).

The prayer, however, seemed no nearer to its

[1] *Cf.* also Isa. l. 7 *ff.*

answer. Jeremiah could point to nothing that
hinted the fulfilment of his scorned and derided
prophecies. Indeed, as we shall see directly, the
stirring events now taking place pointed to the
opposite conclusion. " Why," he asks again, " have
I ever been born ? " (xv. 10–21). " I never tried
to injure anyone, or make money out of my neigh-
bours. Yet I am cursed by all. Have I not
prayed for the very men that despitefully use me
and persecute me ? Then, Jahveh, thy vengeance
on them ! It is not I but thou that art the real
object of their scorn." A momentary gleam of
sunshine flashes across his darkness. " I can
indeed delight in thy word. I am the man who
has received a call from Jahveh of hosts." But it
passes. " No, I am doomed to solitude. Thy hand
is heavy on me all the while. My agony knows no
respite. Thou art no better than a brook that
dries up when its water is most needed ! " On
this note he had ended before ; but now he hears
again the deeper voice, as if all that was best and
firmest in his nature came to consciousness and
announced itself as the very voice of God. " I
have not deserted thee. I still need thee for my
servant. But thy speech must be noble, not
petty. Think not of thy woes, but of my mercy.
Then the real ascendance will be thine, not theirs."
And with this, the old words of the first call return
to his mind. " It will be for thee to fight them ;
but the victory, too, will be thine. A yielding
and timid butt of their jests ? No, a city wall of
bronze. For I will be at hand to rescue, and they
will be powerless against thee."

And was this not the voice of God ? If we

know Jeremiah at all, we know that this is the utterance of the deepest part of him. And what else is the voice of God ? Other men, too, have heard what they called the divine voice. And they have recognised it, not in some new and strange piece of information, but in what they, and we, can feel to be the truths that lie beneath all their thinking and their hopes, the convictions by which they live.

Thus at last comes peace and assurance. The words had been heard long ago ; we remember the recurrence, in more than one crisis, to the mind of the Apostle to the Gentiles, of the words once heard near Damascus. But yet, with Jeremiah, the words were different. The struggles of ten years and more had revealed to him what it meant to be a fortified city and a wall of bronze. He knew what it was to be attacked, and to be victor ; and also to be conscious of Jahveh with him to save him. The years to come were to bring still severer struggles—disappointments and perplexities that might have raised more tyrannous doubts. But, henceforth, he meets them all as a warrior who has won his first campaign. He is not always sure of Jahveh's message ; but, if we may judge from the words whose dates we can assign, he is sure of Jahveh's sincerity and support.

It is impossible to fix the actual date of this victory. The passages which describe the conflict may sum up recurring moods ; and the order which we have suggested may at best be logical rather than chronological. This does not affect the issue of the campaign. Nor does it diminish the light which these remarkable passages throw on the prophetic consciousness. Hitherto, the prophet has been a tool in the hands of Jahveh. What he hears, he must speak. The word is Jahveh's. He has but to repeat it. If Jahveh asks questions, and he replies, it is like the teacher asking and the pupil answering. If the prophet ventures on intercession, it is only for a brief space. But here we see what otherwise we could only have guessed. He, so to speak, stands up against Jahveh. He feels himself to be one independent personality, and Jahveh to be another. Jahveh, who had condescended to plead with Israel through the lips of Isaiah, must now listen to the petulant yet infinitely touching complaints of Jeremiah. What audacity, when dust and ashes should thus rebuke its Creator! In reality, these conversations reveal a new region in the territory of the relations between man and God. God is not the God of tools, but of living men. And if He is to carry the sorrows and sins of His people, He must bear with the doubt and expostulation of His servants. We learn much from Jahveh's answer to Job out of the whirlwind; we learn more when we think of him as listening to all Job's rebellious questioning from his dung-hill.

Until lately, the last thirteen years of Josiah's reign were thought to form a period of peace and security, rudely broken by the disaster of Megiddo in 608. But a recent discovery has thrown an unexpected light on the years which preceded the fall of Assyria, and Judah must have shared the excitement which, as we can now see, kept the whole of Western Asia for years in a ferment. Babylon threw off the Assyrian yoke in the very year after Josiah's reform, and maintained her revolt for four years more. Assyria then entered into an alliance with Egypt, in whose virtual independence she had acquiesced for the last thirty years. By this alliance she hoped to bring the revolt to an end. But Egypt was a long way off, and always more ready to promise than to act. There is for the time no sign of her troops in Mesopotamia.

In the next year, 615, Nabopolassar, the King of Babylon, attacked Ashur, next to Nineveh itself the most important of Assyrian cities, but without success. Then the Medes joined in the mêlée. They had already tried their strength on Assyria in 626, along with the Scythians, and since then they had grown stronger under the wise guidance of their ruler, Cyaxares. In 614 the Medes threatened Nineveh itself, and then turned against Ashur, from which the Babylonian forces had retired, and took it. A counter-alliance was then formed between Nabopolassar and the Medes, cemented by a marriage between Nebuchadnezzar, the Babylonian crown prince, and the daughter of Cyaxares. Nabopolassar in the next season commenced a campaign on the upper Euphrates, but was no more successful than before. He was dislodged by Assyria, and found no help from his new allies. Possibly they were in their turn threatened by the Scythians, who still maintained themselves in Asia, and were always ready to fling their sword now on one side and now on the other.[1] With the Scythians on her side, or only Babylon against her, Assyria might still have held out, and even regained the ground she had lost ; but in 612 Nabopolassar and

[1] Cf. C. J. Gadd, *The Fall of Nineveh* (1923), p. 12.

the Scythians had come to terms, and together their forces attacked Nineveh. The siege lasted two and a half months, from June to August ; and the once proud and cruel mistress of half a continent fell, never to rise again. The shout of relief and triumph that rose from all the countries that had once lived in terror of her arms, and could never forget their fear as long as she still stood, finds a clear echo in the vigorous tones of Nahum.[1]

In these stirring events, Judah played no part. But it was impossible to watch them without suspense. We can imagine the fears in Jerusalem when the news came in 616 that Egypt had decided to assist her ancient suzerain and oppressor ; the hopes when the Medes joined forces with Babylon ; the renewed fears when Assyrian power revived in 613, and the Scythians promised a help which Egypt, on her part, might never actually consent to give. To a period of such oscillation it is tempting to refer one or two striking passages of Jeremiah. In chap. xiv. he describes in the most vivid and moving language the horrors of a drought, when nobles and peasants alike — rich men in the city and their unhappy debtors in the villages—search in vain for water, and the wild animals stand panting for air on the parched hill-tops. But more significant for Jeremiah's own attitude is the passage that follows. The universal misery wrings from him a cry of penitence and supplication. Can it be that Jahveh will sleep while his people are perishing ? " No," comes the answer from Jahveh himself ; " it is no good to intercede for them ; all their ritual is of no avail. All the confidence that

[1] Nahum i. 8 *ff.*

followed Josiah's reform is in vain." "But do
not their prophets still bid them fear nothing ? "
" The prophets " (so Jeremiah goes on, receiving
Jahveh's words in solemn and deliberate prose, in
place of the poetry that had gone before) " are
preaching lies ; and for prophets and people
alike sword and famine shall bring destruction "
(xix. 1–16).

How well (if another conjecture might be
hazarded) this would suit the year of Assyria's
revival, 613. To the same period we might
assign another passage (x. 19–22), when exultation
over the coming fate of Judah is replaced by pity.
Jeremiah feels himself hard hit and broken ; the
politicians are without a spark of true statesman-
ship ; and the air is full of rumours that the attack
of the Northern powers, Assyria and the Scythians,
will at last be let loose on Palestine. Why will
not Jahveh deal with us in measure, he asks, and
pour out his wrath on the heathen who have never
made any pretence of honouring him ?

Once more Jeremiah's anticipations proved false.
The impression made on him at his first call had
prepared him to expect a verification of his
prophecy in every threatening movement from
abroad, especially from the North. What wonder
if his contemporaries treated him as one who was
always ready to cry " Wolf ! " The menace of
613 passed away, and when next year Nineveh was
taken, both the ecclesiastical and the political hopes
in Jerusalem would rise high. The eager though
shallow patriotism that was prone to welcome
every piece of good news as a token of divine favour,
could now speak with an unwonted confidence ;

and Jeremiah, for whom national prosperity—such as it was—had no message, was as isolated as before.

The relief brought by the fall of Nineveh was deep and far-reaching. But it was not complete. A considerable number of the Assyrian forces made their way, under Ashur-uballit, northwards to Harran, and there, in a country called in Nabo-polassar's chronicle Subartu, kept Assyrian power alive. Even yet the old empire might rise again ; all the more, if Egypt were really to come to its help. In the following year, Nabopolassar once more took the field—if we may judge from his chronicle, alone. He invaded the new Assyria in Subartu, but he made no attempt on Harran itself. Next year, however, he was joined by the Scythians, and in the autumn Harran was captured, Asshur-uballit fled, and a garrison of Scythians and Babylonians was left in the town.

But this second piece of good news, great as it was, only raised a new problem for the Judean statesmen. The world was clearly to pass under new masters. But who were they to be ? Cyaxares the Mede, or Nabopolassar ? Or perhaps Egypt ; for Egypt, if she had not yet struck a blow, could not be left out of the reckoning, and was certainly the nearest of the rival powers to Southern Palestine. It was necessary, therefore, that Judah should declare herself. Though the peril of choosing might be considerable, it could not be avoided by the simple expedient of not choosing at all. To Josiah and his statesmen, however, the answer could not be long in doubt. There is much to suggest that the nation was indeed far from being unanimous. Only a few years later, a strong pro-

Egyptian party was to be found in the capital ; and it must almost certainly have existed before. Nor was there difficulty in finding grounds for discrediting the military prowess of Babylon. Moreover, as we shall shortly perceive, the heir apparent, Eliakim, had no leanings to Babylon. Still, opposition to Assyria was a cardinal point in the traditional policy of the court. This would set the country against Egypt. On the other hand, there was a traditional friendship, stretching back over nearly a century, with Assyria's foe, Babylon. True, Babylon had not proved, by herself, a particularly formidable opponent ; but the crown prince, Nebuchadnezzar, was thought to show signs of greater vigour than his father had possessed ; and religion as well as policy forbade Judah to turn to Egypt.[1]

While these resolves were being taken, Egypt decided, at last, to move. In the year after the fall of Harran she sent a force to attack the Scythian and Babylonian garrison in that city. These troops would naturally take the military road through Palestine, along the coast to the plain of Esdraelon, then across the Jordan and so up through Western Gilead into Syria. Judah did nothing. Perhaps the advance took place before Josiah's mind was made up. The Egyptians passed through

[1] In Deut. xvii. 16, the king is forbidden to form connexions with Egypt, though the same code characteristically allows an Eygptian, like an Edomite (xxiii. 8), to be naturalised, on condition of circumcision, in the third generation. Steuernagel *ad loc.* quotes the letter of Aristeas to the effect that Manasseh had been obliged to send recruits to the army of Psamtik ; and finds in Deut. xvii. 16 an allusion to military colonies in Egypt, like the later colony at Aswan.

the country unmolested and laid siege to Harran. Nabopolassar then, it appears, advanced himself, and raised the siege. Egypt was as usual too late to effect anything serious. And Judah, whether the decisive step had been taken before or not, knew herself to be on the side of Babylon.

But Egypt now displayed unaccustomed vigour. Psamtik had died, and his son, Necho, was now on the throne. In the following year, 608, Necho decided to follow up the previous and unsuccessful movement in person. Though Harran was still in the hands of Nabopolassar, the Assyrian cause was not even yet wholly lost ; and a vigorous young Pharaoh was not minded to surrender the rule of Western Asia to Babylon and her allies without a struggle. The fate of the world was to be decided on the Upper Euphrates. But now the time had come when Josiah must act. He had allowed one Egyptian army to pass northwards. He could not allow a second. He collected an army, and chose the plain of Megiddo as the point of his attack. Was there a dream that a second Barak might there defeat another Sisera ? If so, it was not fulfilled. Necho simply brushed his assailant aside, and continued his advance against Babylon and the Scythians, and, as Josephus adds, the Medes.[1] Judah's hopes had risen only to be dashed immediately to the ground. Instead of mounting at

---

[1] Dr A. C. Welch has pointed out (*Expository Times*, January 1924) that the circumstantial narrative of the battle in 2 Chron. xxxv. 20 *ff.* has nothing corresponding to it in 2 Kings xxiii. 29 *ff.*, and asks whether there was really an armed conflict at all, or at least anything more than a skirmish. But how else would Josiah be likely to " go against " Necho ? See also p. 116.

H

last to a new independence under the protection
of Babylon, she had fallen, at the first clash of arms,
before the ally of her old oppressor ; and Josiah,
who of all her kings might have expected and
demanded a victory, returned from the battlefield
to die.

At the moment, perhaps, Necho gave little
thought to the consequences of Megiddo. But
they were fateful for Judah. Unless Necho were
defeated by Nebuchadnezzar on the Euphrates,
a new enslavement was inevitable. It was not a
question now of alliance with either great power.
Judah would be the vassal of the Pharaoh. The
party which had gathered round the crown prince
would be loud in its cry that peace must now be
made with Egypt at once. But the spirit of the
nation, as a whole, like that of the Athenians after
Chæronea, was unbroken. They resolved to pass
over Eliakim in choosing Josiah's successor. They
chose Josiah's younger son, Jehoahaz, as likely to
be truer to his father's ideals, and hoped for the
best. But in vain. Within three months commissioners from Necho had come southwards to
Jerusalem, deposed Jehoahaz, and put his elder
brother in his place. They changed his name from
Eliakim to Jehoiakim (from " God shall set up " to
" Jahveh shall set up ") as if to preserve some
outward continuity with the two preceding kings,
and left him to hold his little country in trust for
Egypt.

VI

THE GAGE FLUNG DOWN

608–597 B.C.

xxii. 10–12, 1–5 (p. 109); xxii. 13–19 (p. 111); vii. 1–14, 21–28; xxvi.[1] (pp. 112 *ff*.); viii. 4–7 (p. 115); xiii. 12–14, 15–17 (p. 115); xviii. 1–12 (p. 118); xix. 1–15 (p. 119); xx. 1–6 (p. 119); xxxvi.[1] (p. 120); xlv.[1] (p. 123); xii. 7–13; xv. 5–9 (p. 124); xxxv.[1] (p. 125); xxii. 24–27, 28–30 (p. 127); xiii. 18–19 (p. 127); ix. (p. 128); xxv. (p. 128).

JEHOIAKIM ascended the throne with a very different programme from that of his father. He was a vassal of Egypt. Nor was he an unwilling vassal. Palestine had no experience of Egyptian devastation such as clung to the memories of the Assyrians; and if, as seemed likely, Babylon should follow the tradition of Assyria in her treatment of subject peoples, it was safer to be under the protection of the Pharaohs. Further, Josiah's policy had been stamped as a failure at Megiddo. Naturally, the new court therefore drew to itself a new set of men. The older statesmen who had surrounded Josiah were still alive, Ahikam, Shaphan, and the rest; but they were discredited and, as we should say, in opposition. Still, they could not be altogether neglected, nor could Josiah's plan be wholly upset. The capital remained a controlling factor in the political situation. It was, as Sir G. A. Smith has called it, the "auditorium" of the nation. And

[1] These sections appear to be from the memoirs of Baruch.

with the importance of the capital was joined the
continued prestige of the temple. So far the
Deuteronomic reform had done its work. The
temple was now, and was to remain, the centre of
the religious life of the nation. But the Puritanism
of the reformers was left undefended. One by one
the old heathen cults crept back into the swept
and garnished chambers of the House of Jahveh.
Political independence had gone; religious independence would have to be surrendered.

The change on the whole was welcomed.
Jeremiah, in a passage which seems to reflect the
popular verdict, speaks of Josiah as a hearty and
jovial monarch, enjoying the good things of life,
and dispensing an even-handed justice to his
subjects.[1] Jehoiakim, in the twelve years of his
reign, was to show a very different character.
Greedy and ostentatious, self-willed and tyrannical,
he had none of his father's virtues. But these
faults had not yet had time to show themselves.
And he had on his side both the priests and the
prophets. Neither of the two great religious
orders in the state, as now became clear, had been
changed by the reformation. The priests were
naturally more interested in the temple rites than
in purity of creed. They had never believed that
Jahveh was a jealous God. Far better that the
temple should offer its hospitality to all who
wished to worship a complaisant divinity than that
the Puritans with their scruples and their icono-
clasm should throw the established religion into a
turmoil. The prophets were all for national survival.
A spirited policy that offered solid hopes of success

[1] Jer. xxii. 15 f.

and shrank from ideals and dreams was sure of their
support. The campaign for moral reformation
had in no age captured the prophetic order as a
whole. Isaiah, Micah, and Zephaniah were the
exceptions, and not the leaders. Even Isaiah, for
all his bitter attacks on the morals of his people,
was convinced that Jerusalem would be preserved ;
and had not the reign of Manasseh vindicated his
conviction ? Lastly, the mass of the people had
been won over. They had put their favourite
Jehoahaz on the throne after Megiddo ; but they
had seen Necho's officers in the capital ; they had
seen Jehoahaz dragged into exile ; they had been
forced to contribute to the " reparations " which
Necho had demanded ; and they were now forced
to respect the *fait accompli*.

What then of Jeremiah ? At first, he would
seem to have been overwhelmed. He has left us
a few passionate words of lament for Jehoahaz,
whom the city was bewailing even before the
mourning for Josiah came to an end. " Weep not
for Josiah," he says in effect ; " he has had his day ;
but weep for the young prince cut off before his
prime. He will never return home " (xxii. 10–12).
Perhaps this announcement of Jeremiah aided the
popular acquiescence in the rule of his less beloved
half-brother. But when the first shock of grief
was over, Jeremiah saw how completely the new
order of things was at variance with himself. With
submission to Egypt he could have nothing to do ;
the temple as a centre of religious worship had no
value for him ; and the idea of national survival
was worthless apart from national morality. From
politicians, priests, and prophets he at once found

himself separated by a great gulf. As long as Josiah was on the throne, there was something with which he could sympathise. Now he was one against the whole nation. Long before this, he has felt himself to be alone. But now his loneliness was different. It was not that alienation from a sordid society which might either oppress or invigorate a generous youth. It was the mature man's clear-sighted recognition that every hope cherished by his country was an illusion.

The effect of this discovery on Jeremiah himself was remarkable. With a lesser man it might have meant despair. Ten years before, he might have despaired himself. But the struggles and the victory described in the last chapter had done their work. Like the " Suffering Servant," whose career seems so strangely joined to his, he has heard the second call, and now opposition itself only serves to strengthen a resolute confidence in Jahveh. Thus, he appears to see his task with a clearness previously unknown. It had been assigned to him twenty years before by Jahveh. And if, like another Elijah, he alone was left, he is possessed by a new determination. He will come out into the open. He will challenge the government of the state. He is prepared for open opposition. He will defy the most powerful interests in the city. It is no longer a matter of impassioned oracles against the debased morals of the country or intrigues among the petty leaders of society in Anathoth. The real enemy of the nation is the king ; and to the king accordingly he must go.

From the period of this discovery dates a new Jeremiah. The poetic inspiration indeed ebbs.

Henceforth we have more prose than verse. He is the preacher or orator, whose duty is to persuade. He has not to think of expressing his own tumultuous convictions, but of changing the convictions of others. Moreover he now begins to resort to symbolic acts, as so many vivid illustrations to enforce his own arguments. He is just as sure as before that what he says and does is given him by Jahveh ; but Jahveh is now the instructor who gives him his lesson and suggests every action in the unremitting yet hopeless task of forcing upon the authorities the stern choice, change of heart or national ruin.

At first, however, Jeremiah did not believe that the task was quite hopeless. In his first appearance before Jehoiakim, he made a simple but authoritative claim for just and benevolent government (xxii. 1–5), every term of which recalls the language of Deuteronomy : the protection of the oppressed, the foreigner, the fatherless, and the widow. " If you show this, your dynasty will be secure and powerful ; if not, your palace will be a ruin." It is the naïve programme of the idealist ; but it is the heart of the traditional Hebrew morality. The message shows no trace of excitement or of the poetic exaltation of the prophecies delivered before 621 ; but it was ignored.

A second message breathes a different tone. What stirred the peasant heart of Jeremiah was the gaudy palace which the king, using forced labour like Solomon his ancestor, had started even in these dark years to build. In words marked by more excitement than before (xxii. 13–19), the prophet asks, " Do you fancy yourself a king because of all this display of cedar wood ? Josiah was a good and honest king ; but you will be buried with the burial of an ass."

Personal appeals to the king were soon perceived to be useless. The next step, therefore, and in reality a bolder one, was to appeal to the people. Accordingly, Jeremiah determined to address the crowd assembled in the temple at a feast—the ancient equivalent of an appeal to the press. Here he had the priests and the prophets to listen to him as well. A definite threat might move them to repentance, and so the coming disaster might be averted. (It is noteworthy that Jeremiah describes this possibility not as his own thought, but as Jahveh's word to him, as if Jahveh shared his uncertainty.) The address, which is summed up in chap. vii. 1–14, 21–28, was sufficiently startling. "What is needed is a reform of your entire conduct. That this place is, as you say, the temple of Jahveh, is nothing. Will Jahveh meet you here if you come to him with hands soiled with theft and murder and hearts foul with adultery and the worship of foreign gods ? That is to turn Jahveh's temple into a den of murderers. Think of Shiloh. You remember its terrible fate. You know the cause. If you persist in a like disobedience, the fate of Shiloh will overtake the temple in which you are standing. Sacrifice as you will, Jahveh never ordered those sacrifices when he gave our fathers the law on Sinai. He demanded obedience ; and that you have never given him." The result might have been expected. We know the result when Jesus was supposed to predict the destruction of the temple of Herod. The dark story of the fall of the shrine at Shiloh has not come down to us. Probably it took place during the early conflicts with the Philistines. The ancestors of Jeremiah himself may well have been priests at Shiloh. Evidently to his hearers it was a symbol of terror and disgrace.

The speech ended in an uproar. The priests had now something definite on which to fix. Jeremiah was at once arrested by them, while the prophets no more recognised him as one of themselves than did the priests. He was brought before the notables, surrounded by an angry mob (chap. xxvi. 1–16, which takes up the narrative of chap. vii.). These notables, rather than the priests or even the king, appear to have had the power of life and death, and before them, and the crowd gathered round them, the priests made their accusation. Confronted thus by the civil power, the priests had to walk a little warily. Jeremiah's offence was subtly changed from sacrilege to treason. It was the city whose downfall he was accused of predicting. Without pausing on this point, he made a simple and dignified reply. " I said what Jahveh told me to say. It is for you to beware of the guilt of killing an innocent man." This impressed his judges and had its effect on the crowd. They were not prepared to deny that they were listening to Jahveh's message. Meanwhile, defence came from another quarter. Some of the leading men from the country who were present, quoted an old prophecy of Micah, uttered about a century before, to the effect that Jerusalem was to be reduced to a ploughed field. In spite of this, Micah had not been executed. But feeling was still very excited, and even then it might have gone hard with the prophet if a member of the older nobility, Ahikam, had not interposed, and carried him off into safety.

The episode is of great value as giving us a glimpse into the internal government of the capital, and its combination of what we should call democracy and aristocracy. Moreover we have here for the first time the description of an incident in the prophet's life, written by an onlooker. The speech in chap. vii. and the account of its sequel in chap. xxvi. are clearly distinct, yet they as clearly refer to the same event. The account has all the vividness of the narratives in the Gospels and Acts. We shall not be wrong in attributing it, like many others that follow, to a friend whom we now find constantly at the prophet's side, Baruch ben Neriah. Jeremiah used him later, as we shall see, as a secretary or amanuensis. He was evidently a skilled writer; possibly Jeremiah himself was not. Jeremiah seems to have found in him what Paul found from time to time in Luke, Silas, Timothy, and the rest. We know no more of his first introduction to the prophet than we know of Luke's introduction to Paul. But he was clearly a man of some position, and we may surmise that this occasion (the first which he narrates) was his first meeting with Jeremiah; perhaps he was present with the nobles, shared their sympathy with the prophet, and then, after his rescue by Ahikam, sought him out and attached himself to him.[1]

---

[1] That Baruch had the entry to the highest circles is clear from chap. xxxvi.; also, chap. li. 59. He was believed later (chap. xliii. 3) to be a pro-Babylonian, *i.e.* to preserve the "aristocratic" traditions of Ahikam and the older nobility of Josiah.

For a time, the danger was past. But it was evident now that in spite of some sympathy in the upper classes, there was no real hope of national repentance. Jeremiah could still plead with those who listened to him (chap. viii. 4–7). " Surely this refusal to repent is against nature. Even the migrant birds, by a divinely planted instinct, know the season for their return ; you have no such instinct ; you only know the blind fury of the war-horse rushing to the battle." On another occasion (chap. xiii. 12–14) he is again in the temple when a feast is being held, and amidst drunken revelry (no wonder that Jeremiah expected little of the protecting sanctity of the temple), the wine-jars are being emptied. " Every wine-jar is to be filled," he cried. The revellers gape at him. " Of course ; but what does he mean ? " " Yes," he continues, " Jahveh will fill you all, kings, priests, prophets, and people, with drunkenness ; and like so many tipsy jars he will set you crashing against one another." Later, in milder tones, he appeals for attention (chap. xiii. 15–17). " Give Jahveh his due honour ; or else you will wander in the darkness, and I shall join my tears to yours."

If we are right in attributing the above addresses to this period, Jeremiah could still appear in public, even after the temple speech. Why did Jehoiakim allow it ? He was not the man to err on the side of mercy. Baruch tells the story of another prophet, Uriah, who had said no more than Jeremiah, but had been obliged to flee into Egypt (xxvi. 20–23). Jehoiakim had demanded his extradition, using as his envoy a member of Ahikam's group, perhaps his own father-in-law,[1] and put him to death ignominiously. The reason may be that though Ahikam and his friends, like Bismarck in his later years, had been dismissed, they exercised an influence which the young king could not as yet afford to despise. But Jehoiakim had other things at the time to occupy his attention. He had to watch what was happening in the North. The Egyptian force had been campaigning in Northern Mesopotamia since 608; but not till 605 was Necho opposed by Nebuchadnezzar the Babylonian crown prince. When the armies met at Carchemish, Necho was decisively beaten (chap. xlvi. 2). This action had for the whole of Western Asia the importance that Megiddo had had for Judah. It meant that Egypt would never again be able to dispute the heritage of Assyria with Babylon. Nebuchadnezzar vigorously followed up his success on the Euphrates; but when he was on the point of invading Egypt, news reached him that his father Nabopolassar had died, and he hastened back to secure the crown. Yet so firmly was his power established that none of the risings usual on the death of an overlord took place. Babylonian supremacy now stretched to the South of Palestine.

Nebuchadnezzar, who is more familiar to English readers from the book of Daniel than from other sources, is generally thought of as a proud and fanatical tyrant. Really, he was one of the first statesmen of antiquity, with an instinct for governing his wide realms of which his Assyrian predecessors had known little. What was he to do with

[1] *Cf.* 2 Kings xxiv. 8.

regard to Jerusalem ? It was always a difficult city to take by storm or siege. Yet he could not afford to leave it in independence, free to intrigue with an enemy, or to hang on the flanks of an army advancing along the coast into Egypt. He decided to bind the awkward little power to Babylon by a solemn oath, and to hope for its loyalty.[1]

But the new Babylonian empire was wide. Judah was at its extremity ; and Jehoiakim, though he had to reconsider his position, might for the time regard himself as practically free. The Egyptian yoke had been raised ; the Babylonian had not begun to press. The temple was still standing. The nation had received a new lease of independence. How absurd, both priests and prophets would argue, to pay any attention to Jeremiah. But with Jeremiah, doubtless better aware of the real strength of Nebuchadnezzar than his opponents, a new conviction began to form. The foe which the nation had sooner or later to fear was actually Nebuchadnezzar. Nebuchadnezzar, therefore, was that foe from the North of which he had been led to prophesy long ago. The words then given him were truer than he had thought. They did not refer to the abortive expeditions of the Scythians, but to a far more formidable enemy, who was still to come.

With such thoughts in his mind, Jeremiah felt himself led to visit a potter's stall ; and as he stood watching the curious inter-play (for such it seemed)

---

[1] 2 Kings xxiv. 1 ; Ezekiel comments bitterly on the Jewish king's subsequent unfaithfulness (xvii. 11–21) ; Cheyne contrasts what he holds to be Isaiah's indifference to Hezekiah's breach of faith with Assyria.

between clay and potter, the clay going wrong and the potter breaking it up and starting afresh, he thought, " how like Jahveh and the nations. If a nation repents, Jahveh will repent too ; but if it goes wrong, it will be broken up " (chap. xviii. 1–12). This came, indeed, as a further revelation from Jahveh ; and it is noteworthy as conveying a suggestion the very opposite of what is usually made by the clay in the potter's hands—the suggestion, that is, of the " free-will " and responsibility of the clay. And as he watched the potter doing his best, hoping that the lump of clay would " behave properly," as we might say, throwing it away with a gesture of disappointment when it did not, and trying again, the prophet saw more deeply into Jahveh's mind. Jahveh was as dependent on the mind of the nation as the potter was on his often intractable material. But he had all the craftsman's longing for a piece of work that would satisfy his requirements. The prophets learnt their theology in strange places.[1]

So strongly did the idea of the pots seize Jeremiah, that he followed it up in another way. He possessed himself of a jar, asking some of the leading men, priests and laymen, to go with him. He left the city by what was known as the pottery gate, leading to the valley of Hinnom, where the city's rubbish was accumulated and destroyed ; an unsavoury place, not only for the refuse which was piled up and blown and scattered about, but because it had

[1] It is pointed out that pottery turned on a wheel was comparatively recent in Palestine ; it is not found before 650. But even to-day bystanders will loiter round a potter's wheel, as round a blacksmith's forge.

been the site of executions, and of the most horrible of Canaanite religious practices, the sacrifice of children. Perhaps Jeremiah had stood there while the ghastly rite was being carried through, watching the struggling children, and listening to the agonised cries of their mothers. The text says that they were sacrificed to Baal; but Jeremiah implies that the parents were offering their children to Jahveh himself (xix. 1–15). In vigorous and biting words, he reveals all the iniquities which the spot suggested, and then smashed his jar into fragments. " So," he added, " shall the city be broken "; and he then left the place, entered the temple, and repeated his sinister prediction there.

Once before he had been in great danger in the temple. Now he is arrested by the head of the temple constabulary, Pashhur ben Immer, who on his own authority places Jeremiah in the stocks, and keeps him there for the night (xx. 1–6).[1] The treatment was painful, and still worse, degrading. It was used for charlatans who pretended to prophetic inspiration (xxix. 26). It would often be convenient to the priests, who had some sort of control over the prophetic guilds, to be able to silence an awkward opponent by saying, " He is a quack or a lunatic; away with him to the stocks." This time none of Jeremiah's friends were there to interpose. In the morning, when he was liberated, he turned upon Pashhur. We can imagine the heated thoughts that had been in his mind through the insupportable night. " You shall be called

[1] The priests, as responsible for public order in the temple, had the right of summary arrest, though not (chap. xxvi. 11) of life and death.

Terror-on-every-side "—a favourite phrase with Jeremiah; "for you and your friends shall go into captivity, and the whole population and all the treasures of the city shall be carried off to Babylon." We have here the first express mention of Babylon. The expectation of the foe from the North was growing clear in his mind.

The next morning saw him once more at liberty. He could not now enter the temple. Yet the need for speaking to the people was as urgent as ever. Convinced as he was at times of the certainty of ruin, he yet felt that no stone was to be left unturned, for securing a repentance that perhaps was even now not hopeless. The lesson of the potter was still in his mind. What could be done? He himself was silenced for the time. But there was a plan. All that he had to say had been said already. The people had not listened. Well, let the message be written down for them. Baruch was at hand, to act as scribe. Accordingly, Baruch was summoned, and Jeremiah dictated to him all the prophecies which he had so far delivered (chap. xxxvi.).[1]

This was a new step in the history of prophecy. The oracles of other prophets had been written down, generally interspersed with biographical details. This is true of Amos, Hosea, and Isaiah. Detached oracles had also been in existence, like

[1] Was everything that Jeremiah had ever said written down, or only a summary? The summary, it would seem, which is also contained in our present book of Jeremiah. Baruch reads the roll three times in one day, so that it could not have been very long; on the other hand, it is quite possible that Jeremiah may have had by him copies of some of his prophecies, from which he could select as he dictated to Baruch. See Appendix II.

the passage preserved in Isaiah ii. and Micah iv., or the prediction quoted from Micah in Jer. xxvi. 18 (see p. 113). Our book of Jeremiah contains a number of such oracles, short pithy sayings, in rhythmical form, which often have very little to connect them either with an author or an occasion. Even we, in a far more literary age, know how often it is easier to remember a quotation than its author or its context. But Jeremiah was contemplating more than a simple collection of his previous utterances. They were not his utterances at all. They were the messages which Jahveh had given him. Possibly, written down, they might do what on his lips they had failed to do.

And what was this ? They might succeed in making it possible for Jahveh not to do what he had it in mind to do. Such, one might say, was the tenderness that dwelt in the midst of all Jeremiah's stern and rugged diatribes. But this was not Jeremiah's own explanation. The desire that Israel might after all be forgiven was not his, but Jahveh's. The whole plan of writing a book that might lead to the disproof of the very assertions it contained, came from Jahveh its author.

Did such an idea, so paradoxical yet so beautiful, really come from Jahveh or was it Jeremiah's ? The question will be discussed later. It is enough here to point out how much is involved in Jeremiah's thought, yearning after an eleventh-hour repentance. It is as if the spirit of Hosea lives again. " How shall I give thee up, Ephraim ? " Or is it an anticipation of the words of Jesus, when even the eleventh hour had passed : " How often would

I have gathered thy children together " ? All
true religion knows that sin and self-will lead
inevitably to destruction, but that the goodness
of God is always leading to repentance.

Baruch then writes the roll; and if we may
credit chap. xxxvi. 9 as compared with chap. xxxvi.
1, keeps it by him for at least nine months, till, on
a special fast-day in the next winter, perhaps on
such a rainy day as that described in Ezra x. 9, the
provincials are assembled along with the inhabitants
of the capital in the temple. He reads it standing
in one of the offices in the temple ; and the son
of the official to whom the room belonged at once
reported the matter to his father, Gemariah.
Gemariah happened to be at the time in another
room, with several other nobles, all of them significantly enough belonging to the " Deuteronomic "
party, though Ahikam, Jeremiah's rescuer on a
former occasion, was not of their number. Baruch
was promptly summoned before them, and bidden
to read the roll again. The effect on them was
like the effect of Deuteronomy on those who had
heard it seventeen years ago ; but Jehoiakim was
not Josiah. " The king must hear this," they said.
Perhaps they thought that it might possibly have
an effect on him also. But they had their doubts.
" You and Jeremiah had better both go into
hiding," they added.

The rest of the story is well known. Jehoiakim
refused to regard the words as Jahveh's at all, or
to think of Jeremiah as inspired. Instead, he
treated the roll with studied contempt, flinging
page after page, as it was read, into the brazier.
The older statesmen protested, but in vain ; and

the king sent three of his own courtiers to arrest
the prophet and Baruch. But by this time they
had safely concealed themselves ; Jahveh, as
Baruch expressed it, hid them.

Jehoiakim's outburst of petulance had as little
result as might have been expected. Jeremiah,
still acting, as he believed, at Jahveh's instigation,
bade his secretary take another roll and write
what proved to be a second and enlarged edition
of the prophecies, with the addition of a special
denunciation of the king. This roll is in all probability the nucleus of our present edition of
Jeremiah's remains.

The contemptuous rejection of his roll by
Jehoiakim could hardly have been wholly unexpected by Jeremiah. But it was a shattering grief
for Baruch. In a pathetic little note which he
attached to his final collection of the prophecies
along with his memoirs (chap. xlv.), he tells us
how, at the writing of the book, he bewailed his
lot, trouble on trouble. He might have known
what to look for when he joined his friend ; but it
was easy for him to suppose that a man of his
influence might maintain his own position and
assist the prophet as well. We may conjecture
that the complaint followed the writing of the
second roll, when the two friends were in hiding
and when the utter hopelessness of the prospect
came home to Baruch.[1] Jeremiah's reply was as
usual felt to come from Jahveh ; and Jahveh

---

[1] It has also been held that this complaint dates from the last
dark days in Egypt (see pp. 175 ff.). But Baruch would be beyond
such laments by that time ; and the future tenses in the text are
against the idea.

spoke to Baruch much as he had answered Jeremiah's complaints in chap. xii. 5 and xv. 19. The times are big with the destruction with which Jahveh will visit the world. They are far too serious for thought of personal advancement. Baruch must be satisfied if, as he is assured, his life is spared. Later on, Baruch was to have many chances of learning that the only wages he or his master could expect were " the wages of going and not to die." He would discover, like the disciples, that he was following a leader who could give him no tangible reward. The close companionship between the two men, unbroken at least till after the melancholy removal to Egypt, eighteen years later, shows how he overcame this burst of disappointment. Baruch is not the least noble of the minor characters of the Old Testament.

For three more years Jeremiah remained in this anomalous position. But in 601 Jehoiakim broke into open rebellion. The rebellion may have been instigated by Egypt ; but Necho was busy within his own frontiers, and Jehoiakim probably knew that no help from the Nile was to be seriously expected. Even then, it would appear, Nebuchadnezzar was slow to take definite steps against him. He contented himself at first with flinging some detachments of his Chaldean army into the country, with other troops from the surrounding nations. But he subsequently gave orders that Jerusalem should be besieged (2 Kings xxiv. 2, 11). All this time, apparently for some five or six years, Jeremiah was silent and in hiding, unless perhaps we attribute to this period such fragments as xii. 7–13 and xv. 5–9. These would indeed well describe the condition of the country while the Babylonian forces were ranging over it, pillaging and destroying, like a flock of wild birds, before the actual siege commenced. But it would seem that during the siege Jeremiah was set at liberty. Possibly the continued imprisonment of one who was held by many to be an inspired prophet created misgivings which at such a time were thought to be more harmful than any words that he might utter.

One incident alone has been preserved by Baruch (chap. xxxv.). When the country was over-run by the Babylonian armies, the country people naturally removed to the shelter of the walls of Jerusalem.[1] Among the rest was a nomad clan, the Rechabites. These Bedouin tribesmen, as we should call them, like others in the wild hills of the Negeb, had become more or less linked with the tribe and the kingdom of Judah, while still pursuing their roving and gipsy-like manner of life. Unlike the bulk of the Hebrews, they rejected all the culture of the Canaanites and refused to touch wine, cultivating no land, and living in tents, the black tents which are still familiar on the fringe of the sown land. Jeremiah was impelled to approach a group of these men, strange and uneasy as they were within the walls of a city, and taking them into one of the side rooms in the temple, to offer them wine. Of course they refused. Then, turning to the by-standers, he went on : " These men have been true, all along, to the command laid on them by their ancestor. Jahveh himself has instructed you as to

[1] *Cf.* Thucydides' description of the removal of the farmers of Attica into Athens in the early hostilities of the Peloponnesian War, bk. ii. 52.

his will for you ; and you have paid no attention at all. Therefore, all the warnings you have received will be fulfilled upon you ; but the clan of the Rechabites will never die out.''

During the siege, Jehoiakim's tempestuous reign came to an end. Long ago, Jeremiah had prophesied that it would end in ignominy (xxxvi. 30, xxii. 19 ; *cf.* 2 Kings xxiv. 5). The actual manner of the king's death is not known.[1] We cannot say whether Jeremiah's prediction was fulfilled or not ; probably Jeremiah would have been little interested in the precise fate of Jehoiakim's dead body. He may, as Cheyne suggests, have been assassinated, like Amon, and buried by stealth. He was not an apostate. He was true, according to his light, to what was implied by his name. He worshipped Jahveh, as did all his subjects. His fault was that his Jahveh was a false Jahveh, a being who did not really exist, one who was content to overlook injustice, oppression, lust, self-seeking, if only worship and prayer were sedulously offered, and who could be relied upon, in the last event, to let the will of his worshippers be done. In such a Jahveh the majority of Israel believed, from first to last. Amos and Hosea, Isaiah and Jeremiah, knew that Jahveh was very different from this. That was their message for their own time. Has it lost its importance to-day ?

The death of Jehoiakim changed nothing. His young son Jehoiachin or, as he is also called,

---

[1] In 2 Chron. xxxvi. 6, 8, Jehoiakim is carried in fetters to Babylon ; the Septuagint adds that he was buried with his fathers " in Ganosae," apparently a misreading of a notice that he was buried in the garden of Hosea.

Coniah, was at once placed on the throne. Coniah
was a lad of only eighteen years old,[1] and it was
natural that his mother and the men who had
surrounded Jehoiakim should continue to guide
the desperate affairs of the invested city. The
only hint as to the feeling in Jerusalem is to be
found in a brief oracle of Jeremiah (xxii. 24–27).
" Though Coniah were the signet-ring on my
finger, Jahveh hath said, I would tear him off and
fling him away, and his mother with him ; and they
will die in Babylon." But even without this
sinister prediction, the spirit of the defenders was
already broken ; Jeremiah speaks in the same
oracle of Coniah's fear ; and after a brief interval
of three months, the king and the court surrendered to Nebuchadnezzar. It was the tragedy of
Jehoahaz re-enacted (*cf.* xxii. 10 ff.). The youth
was dragged away almost before he had learnt to
wear his crown. Jeremiah had lamented the fate
of the uncle, and now a sharp outburst of grief
followed the equally harsh fate of the nephew
(xxii. 28–30). " Was Coniah nothing but a cheap
household pot, that he should be flung aside like
that ? " Yet no indignant sorrow over the past
could veil the certainty of the future. With his
fall came the fall of his house. The line of David
had existed for four hundred years in Jerusalem ;
it would exist no longer. Coniah would have no
child to mount the throne. Another fragment of
a lament is found in xiii. 18, 19.

The prophecy, it has often been pointed out,
was not literally fulfilled. Coniah did not die
childless ; the name of his son is given in the

---

[1] 2 Kings xxiv. 8.

genealogical tables as Salathiel ; and it is probable that Salathiel's son was Zerubbabel, was who at the head of affairs in Jerusalem when Cyrus had given permission to the exiles to return. Indeed, it was through Coniah that the line of David was extended to Jesus. But Jeremiah's assertion that no descendant of Coniah would ever sit on the throne of David was certainly borne out. Regarded as king, Coniah was childless ; and it is perhaps remarkable that Jeremiah was actually correct as regards the fate both of the father and the son. Others might believe in Coniah's return ; we shall find that they did. Jeremiah had no such illusions (*cf.* pp. 132 *ff.*). And the intensity with which he voiced his announcement, " earth, earth, earth, listen to the message of Jahveh," shows how deeply his spirit was stirred, at once by sorrow and by renewed assurance.

The clashing emotions that struggled in Jeremiah's mind through these stormy years can be studied in ch. ix. (with the exception of the later vv. 7, 8, 11, 12, 26). Distress, condemnation, divine judgment, lament, and eager piety ; here are the key-notes of all Jeremiah's hourly-varying moods. It is as impossible as it is needless to try to date the passages with exactness : but to the same period (doubtless the earlier portion of Jehoiakim's reign) must be assigned the stern words of xxv. 1–10, to which three appendices (not very germane) were subsequently added (vv. 11–14 ; 15–31 ; 32–38 ; note specially v. 13, and see p. 215).

VII

THE TWO PATRIOTISMS

597–588 B.C.

xxiii. (p. 134); xxiv. (p. 135); xxix. 1–23 (p. 136); xxix. 24–32 (p. 137); xiii. 1–11 (p. 138); xxvii. (p. 139); xxviii.[1] (p. 140).

CONIAH's surrender did not bring the existence of the city to an end. Nebuchadnezzar had summed up the situation in Jerusalem for himself, and it would appear that his estimate of the strength of Jeremiah's political friends led him to falsify, for the time, Jeremiah's predictions. He did not give up hope, even now, of the city's loyalty. To destroy it would be to remove what might still turn out to be a valuable obstacle in the way of any advance of Egypt. He did not identify the country as a whole with the anti-Babylonian party. The irreconcilable hostility of the court and the government he felt it necessary to remove ; and a rigorous measure of disarmament was also an obvious precaution. With the king and the royal family therefore he transferred to Babylon all the leading members of the military and influential classes, as well as the more important craftsmen. The survivors, as he evidently hoped, would have neither the skill nor the experience to organise a formidable army, nor the means to equip it. 2 Kings puts the deported in round numbers at 8000. With

[1] From Baruch's memoirs.

them would go their families ; from 30,000 to 40,000 would perhaps represent the total. The population of Jerusalem at the present time is about 64,000, and the population of the whole kingdom of Judah in Jehoiakim's time numbered possibly rather more than 200,000. The deportation was therefore a serious matter, in numbers as well as in quality.[1] We hear nothing of any extensive looting of the city, but many of the sacred vessels of the temple were removed—a disgrace which was deeply felt.

Nebuchadnezzar took care, however, that there should be material for carrying on the government of the state. He placed on the throne a half-brother of Jehoiakim—Mattaniah ("gift of Jahveh"), whose name was thereupon changed to Zedekiah ("righteousness of Jahveh") ; and some at least of the party of the "men of 621" were left with him. We hear no more of Ahikam ; but Gedaliah his son remained, and doubtless after this drastic "purge" Nebuchadnezzar hoped that he would have little trouble with Jerusalem, and that he could indeed allow the city much of its old independence.

The new king, Zedekiah, the last of his line, is one of the most pathetic figures in Hebrew history. He had solemnly pledged himself to be loyal to Babylon, and he appears to have been honestly anxious to keep his word. But it was soon evident that loyalty to Babylon was the last thing desired by the new men who surrounded him ; and he

---

[1] See footnote on p. 166. The numbers given in Kings and in Jeremiah do not tally. Perhaps Kings refers to the whole kingdom of Judah and Jeremiah to the capital.

proved too weak to resist. Dragged into rebellion against the king he had sworn to obey, and relentlessly opposed by Jeremiah, whose assurance of Jahveh's favour and protection he secretly longed for, without a friend or a minister whom he could trust, without a policy that he dared to carry through, forced to condemn the very man whom he at once admired and feared, he was driven to a fate that he would gladly have warded off, but which his own weakness made inevitable.

Meanwhile, Jeremiah found himself in a new position. His strongest friends and his most determined foes were gone. Jehoiakim himself was gone ; so were the men who had surrounded him. The new king was at all events disposed to be friendly. And the deportation of so many of the leading citizens had left him at least relatively with much more influence. Amidst the crowd of untried men who now had the city's destinies in their hands, his experience of national life for nearly thirty years was something to be reckoned with. He was not now a voice crying in the wilderness, as in the early days before the Deuteronomic reformation, or even when under Jehoiakim he was a declared opponent of the entire policy of the king. Accordingly, he now gave himself less than before to public preaching. Years, too, and the strain with which those years had been filled, were beginning to tell on him. For declamation at the street corner he seems now to have neither spirit nor strength. If protests are needed now, they will have to be made directly to the men who are influencing national action and policy. The result is that we know more about him in the next

eleven years than in any other period of his life.
Had he confined himself to the prophesying that
had filled his earlier years, we should have known
little of his dealings with his contemporaries. On
the other hand, had he lived alone as he had done
previously, we should probably have known nothing.
But Baruch was now constantly at his side, and
from the memoirs of Baruch we can trace his life
through the troubled reign of Zedekiah. For the
activity that was now demanded of him was just
what Baruch was fitted to describe. Thanks to
Baruch, with the help of the brief records of the
books of Kings, we are more at home in Jerusalem
under Zedekiah than at any earlier time.

The first thing that Baruch makes clear is the
remarkable power of recuperation in the little
Hebrew state. Whether Nebuchadnezzar had gone
as far in stripping the city of its defences as the
book of Kings implies, the state acts from the first
as if it were fully able to stand on its own feet.
Not less remarkable was its tone of confidence.
Nebuchadnezzar had not transplanted all the
prophets to Babylon. Perhaps he was not aware
of the popular influence which the prophets
exerted. He may have despised them. A foreign
conqueror in more modern times might easily
under-rate the influence of the clergy among a
superstitious and high-spirited peasantry. But the
bulk of the prophets were from the beginning
quite convinced that the measures of Nebuchadnezzar in 597 amounted to nothing more than a
temporary set-back. The exiles would return.
The temple vessels would be restored. The city
would rise more glorious from its shame. How,

indeed, we might ask, could religious faith have expected anything else ? Was not Jahveh bound to protect his own property and defend his own glory ? Would he not show that his power was far above that of even the proud victor of Babylon ? We can easily see how such questions would appeal at once to the patriotism and the religion of Israel. Moreover, the prophets might ask, had not the city been purified ? The wickedness and idolatry of Jehoiakim's reign had come to an end. The city had come back to the obedience and purity which Jahveh was bound to reward. The crowning mercy of 701 was now to be repeated.

Further, the men now in charge of Jerusalem seem to have regarded themselves as well rid of the exiles. " Abraham was one single man, and Jahveh gave him the land. We are few, and the land is ours." " This city is the cauldron, and we are the good meat in it." [1] Doubtless, the exiles would return ; but meanwhile, the city was quite capable of looking after itself. The exiles were well aware for their part of what was going on in Jerusalem. Once arrived in Mesopotamia, they were able to form communities of their own, and to organise some sort of social and commercial life. They too had their prophets, who were convinced of the certainty of a speedy return. But they were by no means disposed to undervalue themselves, or to suppose that the survivors in Jerusalem were necessarily the most fitted to survive. They too had their faith in Jahveh,[2] and when they returned, it

---

[1] Ezek. xxxiii. 24 ; xi. 3.

[2] The book of Ezekiel shows that their faith needed purifying as much as did the faith of the Jerusalemites.

would be through the might of Jahveh and not through any virtue on the part of those who had been left at home.

But all this betokened an attitude with which Jeremiah could have no sympathy. The city had indeed for the time escaped its doom. But the spirit which would bring down that doom upon it was still there. Nothing but a change of heart could avert destruction ; and what hope was there of that ? The prophets, Jeremiah felt, were still at their old task of buoying up fallacious hopes with a pretended inspiration. In chap. xxiii. we have a collection of oracles levelled at these prophets. Uttered in all probability at different times, they reveal a mind which knows that the prophets are wrong, and yet has not thought out the whole case against them, nor indeed become conscious of the real grounds of its conviction. " They have not stood in Jahveh's counsels, nor listened to his decrees. They assume that all will be well—proof enough that they are impostors. They tell of their dreams ; let them speak out plainly if they have any divine message. They simply steal their words from one another, repeating parrot-fashion what their leaders have chosen to say. They talk incessantly about the ' burden of Jahveh.' Jahveh will treat them and their lies like a burden, as they call it, and will throw them off his shoulders." [1]

Jeremiah had not yet done with the prophets,

---

[1] A grim and characteristic play on words. We talk about the " burden " of a speech or a message. The phrase was familiar in Israel ; *cf.* Isa. xiii. 1, etc. But the prophets were turning themselves into a burden to Jahveh, which he was no longer willing to bear.

nor with the real difficulty of prophetic inspiration. He might be sure that their inspiration was a sham ; they might affirm with equal confidence that it was he who was lying.   By what criteria could he prove his point or the public decide ?   The question arises whenever men claim to prophesy, and each prophet has to find his answer.   Meanwhile, the towering self-confidence of the people as a whole had to be rebuked.   To Jeremiah, even though the company of exiles contained so many who were personally hostile to himself, there was no doubt that it contained the flower of the nation.   Was there, we may perhaps ask, a tendency to idealise them when in their absence they were contrasted with the crew now laying their uncertain hands on the rudder ? His eye was caught, possibly when passing the collected offerings of first-fruits in the temple, by two baskets of figs, the one as bad as the other was good (chap. xxiv.).   They at once suggested to him the contrast between the exiles abroad and the survivors at home.   In its present form, Jeremiah's comment contains a prediction that the exiles would receive the gift of a new mental attitude from Jahveh, and would return, while the community in Jerusalem as well as those who had sought safety in Egypt, would be scattered to the winds.   It has been urged that Jeremiah's own words have been overlaid with a later addition, though it is not clear when such an addition would have been made.

Subsequently however Jeremiah's view of the future grew clearer.   These predictions of return, uttered in both sections of the nation, and the unrest and excitement that would naturally follow them, would not escape the vigilance of the Baby-

lonian authorities; and it became advisable for
Zedekiah to dissociate himself from them, and to
give some proof of his loyalty. Accordingly, he
sent a mission to Babylon, headed by two members
of the 621 party, and Jeremiah seized the occasion to
send a message of his own to the exiled community
(xxix. 1–23), in which he stated very explicitly that
the Jews in Babylonia were to reconcile themselves
to a long sojourn there, to settle down, in fact, and
to act as good citizens in their new home.[1] Not
till two generations had passed would their return
take place. Then Israel would call and Jahveh
would answer, while the bad figs would be flung
far away. Jeremiah then turns upon two of his
opponents among the prophets in Babylon, and
with a vehemence that reminds us of his attack
upon Pashhur, tells of their coming execution by
Nebuchadnezzar. He accuses them of scandalous
immorality. If Nebuchadnezzar punished them, it
would be for political agitation.

This letter produced a counterblast. Opinion
among the exiles was by no means unanimous. On
the one hand there were those who were quite in
agreement with Jeremiah, convinced that the city's
doom was sealed, and that any return to Palestine
was for the time at least impossible. Among these
was the prophet Ezekiel. Throughout the reign
of Zedekiah, he reiterated the guilt of the city and
of the whole nation in even more lurid terms than
Jeremiah, using all the artifices of symbol and

---

[1] Jeremiah uses the round number of seventy years. The
exact figure is not to be pressed, though from the actual year in
which he is writing, probably 595, to the accession of Cyrus, was
just sixty years.

from Jahveh. And if those who watched them thought their conduct insane, they had been brought up to regard insanity, too, as Jahveh's work.

For us, however, as for Jeremiah himself, the reference of an overmastering impulse to the direct action of Jahveh raises once more the question—if contrary impulses come to different persons, what then ? We are already familiar with the fact that Jeremiah was not the only prophet in Jerusalem, and that the larger number of prophets were entirely out of sympathy with him. Four years after Zedekiah's accession thay sprang into fresh activity. A new King of Egypt came to the throne in 593, Psamtik II. A change of monarch always meant a possibility of political disturbance. Psamtik's accession was the signal for a hasty anti-Babylonian coalition in Western Asia. The old rivals of the nation, Edom, Ammon, and Moab, and the Phœnician states of Tyre and Sidon, whose traditional alliance with the Hebrews had not been forgotten, united ; and with Judah and the important city of Jerusalem to support them, and the might of Egypt behind, Nebuchadnezzar could safely be defied. Accordingly, envoys were sent to Zedekiah, and they found an eager welcome among the men who surrounded the king. The prophets, true to their nationalistic ideals, saw in this invitation the hand of Jahveh. The god of their fathers had chosen this alliance to deliver his people, and the suzerainty of Babylon would come to an end.

Jeremiah knew better. Once more he was alone. But he was undaunted. Left to his own thoughts, he might waver. He found a clear call in the need for action (chap. xxvii.). In this instance, the real foes were the foreign envoys. He appeared before them bending under the weight of a heavy yoke, such as would be carried by two oxen at the plough, and he bade them tell their masters that the yoke of Nebuchadnezzar was to rest upon them all, in spite of every prediction to the contrary, and that they had best submit. He carried the same message to the court of Zedekiah, and then turned to the priests and bade them relinquish all hope that the captured temple vessels would be brought back. " Your prophets," he added grimly, " would be far better employed in praying for the safety of the vessels which are left here."

If the envoys were influenced by inspired predictions (and they would not have been men of their age if they had not been), they would naturally pay more attention to the chorus of acclamation which assured success to their hopes than to the solitary voice which told of calamity. But in Jerusalem itself Jeremiah could not be ignored. Baruch's story of the event reminds us closely of the older story of Micaiah, who opposed the whole guild of prophets in Samaria when Ahab was proposing his ill-fated expedition against Ramoth-Gilead, two hundred and fifty years before. In neither story is the prophet believed ; in both he awakens an uneasy feeling (natural enough in moments of tension and nervousness) that he may be right after all. But at this point Baruch's story takes a shape which casts an unexpected light on the inner thought of his hero (chap. xxviii.). Hananiah, one of the government or orthodox prophets (we may call him either as we think more of the political or the religious side of his ministry), came upon Jeremiah in the temple, surrounded by the priests and the crowd, and still stooping under his ridiculous yoke. He had given his message. No one had supported him. We do not know that even Baruch was wont to appear at his side in public. Perhaps the old doubts had arisen again. Was he really right ? Was the city's doom so certain ? Then came Hananiah. He too had his word from Jahveh. " Two years, and the temple vessels will be back in their place here ; Jehoiachin will be back in his palace yonder, and the yoke of Nebuchadnezzar," he added, pointing to Jeremiah's burden, " will be broken."

Baruch's concise but vivid narrative lets us see Jeremiah's hesitation ; a hesitation all the harder to resist, perhaps, because of the physical weariness from the weight he was carrying. " So be it," he said ; " nothing could be more welcome to me. But remember that in the past Jahveh's messages have always been of disaster." We can imagine the vigorous signs of dissent from the prophets here. " Such a prophecy as yours will be attested by the event." Hananiah saw his evident perplexity, and with a conviction that contrasted strongly with his opponent's doubt, he made for him, tore the yoke from his neck, and broke it with his own hands. The feat was a startling one, reminding the bystanders of what other prophets had done when the spirit of Jahveh was on them ; and, carried along by his frenzied confidence, he repeated his prediction that within two years the yoke of Nebuchadnezzar would be smashed like the fragments he held in his hands. Jeremiah silently retired.

But that was not the end. In a few days,

perhaps a few hours, Jeremiah was back. The ebbing tide had turned. Hananiah could not be right. Jeremiah knew Jahveh too well. All this talk of two years and then recovery was a lie. The wooden yoke might be broken. Jahveh's yoke was an iron one, which none could break, and which would bring all the nations into slavery to Nebuchadnezzar. Hananiah, like Pashhur and Shemaiah, would die, and within a year. Baruch adds that Hananiah actually did die long before the year was out. This need not surprise us; nor need we suppose that Jahveh took this means of accrediting his servant after a sufficient but not too long interval. Among Orientals, as among primitive peoples, a curse, like a broken taboo, may bring of itself the most serious results. But, unless we assume that the matter was merely a coincidence, we can see that there was something in Jeremiah which compelled attention to his words; or perhaps he impressed his hearers by his obvious disinterestedness. No one could suppose that he had any selfish end to serve, even his own personal safety, by his outspoken assertion of statements that turned every one against him.

At bottom, they knew that he was right, as he knew that they were wrong. The criterion was a moral one. The court where the question was to be decided was the court of conscience. Jeremiah had not yet come to the point where he could state this explicitly. He simply saw that all genuine predictions in the past had been predictions of woe, and that therefore any prediction of prosperity must justify itself by the event. On the surface, this seems a terrible doctrine.

Must we take it for granted that God will send a curse unless we are forced to admit, in some specific instance, that he has actually sent a blessing? If we make this a general statement, it is false. If we apply it to Israel, Jeremiah at least would assert it to be true. For the history of Israel was one long record of neglect, defiance, infidelity. A god who could ask from Israel any gift save repentance or bestow any blessing save the new and repentant heart, was no god at all. That was the message of Jeremiah; and it is the message without which the gospel itself is either misunderstood or parodied. What was the work of Christ save the opening of a way to give this new heart? Jeremiah never saw, as the author of the Servant poems did see, the awful passion through which that gift of the new heart was to be communicated. But no one in the history of Israel came nearer to that passion than Jeremiah.

And now for one word on Hananiah. Most readers will find Jeremiah's attitude to Hananiah, Pashhur and the rest, the least tolerable thing about him. Granted that his death, psychologically, was like the death of a savage against whom a venerated witch-doctor has woven a spell or uttered a magic word, did he deserve to die? Was he not one of those eager souls who refuse to believe, in time of war, that a good God could give up his people to defeat? "Do not tell us of our sins," such men will say. "At all events, they are not as bad as the sins of our enemies. We have faith in God, and we will not surrender it. This new alliance is providential. A few more months, and by the grace of God we shall have won the war."

Such was doubtless Hananiah's argument. It is familiar enough to many persons to-day. Where was the lie ? It was, as Plato would have said, in the heart. It was not a conscious falsehood. They were not deliberate deceivers who, on either side, spoke of the "God of our fathers," during the European war. It was something worse. Tried by the standard of Jeremiah, the eyes of their understanding were blinded. They were all in the dark about God. They did not know that He cared about one thing and one thing only ; that combination of straight dealing, kindliness and reverent obedience which had been the demand of all the great prophets of the opposition from Amos to Zephaniah. And therefore they did not know that a society which had no mind to produce these fruits could receive no gift at all from God, and must therefore in such circumstances as surrounded Judah come to destruction. And with Judah destruction did follow. We can see now that with conduct such as hers, and so powerful an enemy to be defied, nothing else could have happened. Destruction does not always follow upon the mind which possessed Judah, and against which Jeremiah raised his protest in vain History has made that plain to us. But if victory should come instead of the defeat that Jeremiah prophesied as the only possible result for so misunderstanding God, that victory may be in itself worse than a defeat. Better no victory at all than a victory which should slowly stifle a nation's soul. History has furnished abundant examples of such victories, and their results.

Hananiah's lie was founded on ignorance. But the ignorance was wilful. He ought to have known.

He could have known. Whether he deserved his fate is a question we need not decide. When can we, with our imperfect knowledge, ever say that a man's fate is deserved or not ? It is more important for us to observe the striking modernity of the whole controversy, and to remember that to Jeremiah, as to every writer in the New Testament, the will of God is not that we should receive any specific political or economic blessing, but that we should change our attitude to life and believe the good news that we can become the children of God, the Father in Heaven.

VIII

JERUSALEM DELENDA

588–586 B.C.

xxxiv. 1–7 [1] (p. 153); xxi. 1–10 [1] (p. 154); xxxii. (p. 155); xxxiv. 8–20 [1] (p. 158); xxxvii. 3–10 [1] (p. 161); xxxvii. 17–21 [1] (p. 162); xxxviii.[1] (pp. 163 *ff.*); xxxix.[1] (p. 165); xl.[1] (p. 167).

WHATEVER Hananiah and his friends expected, they were diasppointed. Psamtik II. was not another Necho. He was more interested in Nubia than in Palestine. No troops came up from Egypt, and the coalition achieved nothing. Zedekiah was thus free from the guilt of a formal breach of his oath to Babylon. But Psamtik died four years after his accession, and Hophra, or Apries as the Greeks called him, took his place. Hophra was a monarch of a different stamp. Eager to regain the glories of the great Pharaohs of a bygone age, he had his eye on Syria; and in spite of the Egyptian defeat at Carchemish twelve years ago, the position of Nebuchadnezzar was not so sure that a few bold moves might not upset it. Palestine was nearer to Egypt than to Babylon; and the events of Psamtik's reign had shown how widespread was the disaffection to the Babylonian government in Western Asia.

Hophra's suggestions were eagerly listened to by the statesmen in Jerusalem. Zedekiah himself

---

[1] From Baruch's memoirs.

suffered all the misery of the mind that faces both ways. But his ministers knew what they wanted and meant to have it. Nationalism is often discussed as if it were a growth of quite modern times. But the contemporaries of Jeremiah would have had no great difficulty in understanding at least some of the ideals of Swaraj or Sinn Fein. As regards the economic and social sides of nationalism, they had no more idea of expelling Babylonian civilisation than India, save for a few extremists, has of expelling the machinery of Western education. To the religious cults of Mesopotamia, the Hebrews showed a hospitality that India has never showed to Christianity. But in politics there was the same determined resolve to get rid of the foreigner. The Hebrews could not, like India or the Egypt of to-day, pride themselves on a national life which was old when the foreigners in their midst were little better than savages. But they were as resolute in turning from the realities of the present to the dreams of the future. It was nothing to them that Babylon, like the British Empire, possessed resources which they could hardly imagine ; that the strong hand of Babylon would keep a peace which would be for the advantage of every one, and that if her troops and her officers were driven back to the Euphrates, Western Asia would again, as we say, be Balkanised. Worse than that (though this might not have seemed a drawback to the ruling classes), there would be all the opportunities for social conflict and the exploitation of the poor by the rich that had disgraced the eighth century.

On the other hand, the motives for resistance were quite intelligible. The confidence of Hananiah, though to Jeremiah it was founded on a lie, had within it, as we have seen, an element of religious faith. Hananiah had behind him all the early traditions of the nation, found, for example, in the older documents of the Pentateuch known as J and E ; and he could have appealed with assurance to Deuteronomy. Had not the law given to Moses been put into operation, and had not Jahveh sworn to their fathers to give them the land as a reward for their obedience to its demands ? Josiah indeed had fallen at Megiddo, but that, one might well argue, was a consequence of his rash opposition to Egypt and his willingness to co-operate with Babylon. All the more reason, surely, for accepting the proffered help of Egypt now and preparing to throw off the Babylonian yoke. If Isaiah had prophesied the downfall of the despotic city on the Tigris, a prophecy which had been so strikingly fufilled in their own days, was it not Jahveh's will to visit with a like doom her successor on the Euphrates ?

Such arguments would add fuel to the fire of the national love of independence, always strongest in a generous people when most severely threatened ; and if it was easy to think of Babylon as the tyrant, hated by Jahveh, it was equally easy to forget how quickly her place might have been taken by Egypt, or even by Judah's ally on the sea-coast, Tyre.[1]

[1] It is noteworthy that in Ezekiel's prophecies against foreign nations, which date from this period, he passes very rapidly over Moab, Edom, and the rest, but exhausts the powers of his imagination in dealing with Tyre and Egypt. Babylon is not mentioned. But the attitude to Babylon of Second Isaiah and the author of Jeremiah l., li. (see p. 215), may well have been shared by seriously-minded Hebrews before the fall of Jerusalem.

What is really surprising is that the men left in charge of Jerusalem by Nebuchadnezzar in 597 should have surrendered to these arguments so completely. They surely might have been expected to see that for them continuance in power meant loyalty to the sovereign to whom they owed their place. This was doubtless what Nebuchadnezzar had intended by his dispositions. He meant Gedaliah and his friends to have their chance. But they did not get it. The men who gained control of affairs were men who carried on the policy of the last years of Jehoiakim. By forcing the pro-Babylonians into opposition they burnt their boats. They could only hope to remain in power so long as Babylon was kept at a distance. Meanwhile, however, they had both priests and prophets with them. Nationalism and cultus were both on the side of opposition to Babylon; and by a strange irony the successors of the " men of 621 " found all the influence of the memory of that reformation on the side of their opponents, and they had to watch Josiah's son terrorised into a weak compliance with their enemies.

The situation was serious, and Nebuchadnezzar determined to meet it at once. For the politics of his empire, Palestine was only a pawn in the game. His real objective, and the source of his real danger, was Egypt. If he had had to deal with Palestine by itself, or even with Palestine and the neighbouring states, he would have brushed aside this opposition as quickly as Necho had done at Megiddo. But history had taught the Mesopotamian powers that even if they did not contemplate subduing Egypt, they could never be safe so long as Egypt had a free hand to spread disaffection in Palestine and Syria, and could thus send her troops to the Upper Euphrates. Palestine, therefore, though a pawn, was a very important one, and Jerusalem, though it lay off the main military route, was one of the keys of the situation. If Jerusalem was hostile, the line of communications along the coast road would always be insecure, and Egypt could never be attacked with any real hope of success. On the other hand, if Jerusalem were held by a Babylonian force, Egyptian troops could be effectively prevented from advancing northwards.

Accordingly, an army was despatched into Palestine, and siege was laid to the turbulent little city. The Hebrews did not venture to meet their enemies in the field. Instead, the population of the surrounding country once more crowded into the city streets. Before repeated invasions had disorganised the country, the walled towns had served as a refuge both for the agricultural peasants and their stock in any emergency. Indeed, a large part of the population regularly lived in the towns and worked in the fields. But when, under a more definite attack, every one was driven into the capital, grave difficulties arose. Overcrowding (a feature, as the excavators have shown us, of all Oriental town life) would be painfully increased ; disease would quickly break out when animals and men were herded together in a town where a regular water supply (save for one rather unsatisfactory conduit) was unknown ; and food would soon begin to run short. Nervous tension would increase every week. In such an atmosphere anything might be expected.

But the siege lasted two years. However desperate the conditions, the population set themselves to the task of resistance with rare heroism. It would seem indeed that there is something in the circumstances of a prolonged siege which may bring out latent powers of self-control and courage. Platæa, Saragossa, and Ladysmith tell the same tale. And for these two years, the memoirs of Baruch are exceptionally full. He did not compile them in order to inform us as to the state of affairs in Jerusalem, any more than Luke intended to tell us about Roman administration in the provinces. But his narrative throws a vivid light on life in a city-fortress subject to the stress of a prolonged siege, and when we can place ourselves in the city and watch the men who were in power there, we can appreciate far more fully the position of Jeremiah himself. Baruch writes, too, as one who knew the life of the city intimately. He does not deal with groups, but with individuals : the secretary of state, Jonathan, who had a sort of *oubliette* in his perhaps official residence ; the blunt and slow-witted soldier, Irijah, in the guard-house ; and the negro Ebed-melech, whose human sympathies had not been killed off by political anxieties. Baruch knew them all ; and sometimes he appears to mention names for the mere love of mentioning them, like the author of the Fourth Gospel.

Jeremiah was now an old man. The rhythmical addresses and the sermons of the earlier years have come to an end ; there was probably no opportunity, and no permission, in the abnormal condition of things, for their delivery. Very likely Jeremiah had no physical strength to utter them, and no hope for results from them. Even in the

previous reign they had been growing rare. He
could see the end, if others could not. The foe
from the North was not now threatening his dreaded
attack. He was already at the gates. The bravest
of the defenders would soon be thinking that
nothing was left save to sell their lives as dearly as
possible. A less passionate or more self-centred
man than Jeremiah might have now been content
to say, " I told you so," and to watch quietly for
the end. All through his life hitherto, his predictions, as we have seen, had somehow missed fire.
He had felt himself deceived, " seduced." Now
all was coming true. In his country's ruin, his own
prophetic credit at least might triumph.

Jeremiah, however, was not a man of this stamp.
His own prophetic credit was nothing to him. But
the safety of Jerusalem, though it might be nothing to Jahveh apart from repentance and moral
integrity, was everything to him. Long before
this, he had dreaded the awful silence in which the
pleasant sounds of the household mill-stones and
the voice of the bridegroom and the bride would
be stilled. Hosea in similar circumstances had felt
his own dread projected into the mind of Jahveh.
Not so with Jeremiah. He might plead ; Jahveh
only rebuked his pleadings. The mercy was in the
thoughts of the man ; the sternness in the heart of
God. Yet, by a sublime inconsistency, Jeremiah
would not be content with this. He would not
give up hope. Could there be a moment when
warnings would be too late ? Sometimes he
answered " Yes," sometimes, " No." And because
he was so sure that such warnings could not be
unavailing, he felt himself constrained by Jahveh

to utter them.[1] His convictions triumphed over his logic. The stern and simple indicative, " You will perish," changed again and again into a milder conditional, " If you do not repent, you will perish," and this again into another, " If you will turn, you may yet be saved " : and even, now and then, into the actual promise, " The repentant heart will be given, and then restoration will follow."

Such were the moods that alternated in the mind of Jeremiah during those tense months of siege. Each alternative he interpreted as a fresh message from Jahveh. Those who listened to him might well have been perplexed. They might have told him, as Hananiah did, that Jahveh had not spoken by him. But he was his own most drastic, though quite unconscious critic. And as hope succeeded fear, and certainty succeeded hope, he felt every new emotion and gust of feeling as another movement of Jahveh within him. He was the prophet of Jahveh to the end, to pull down and to build up.

Was he right ? This we must consider later. Meanwhile, at the very beginning of the siege, while Nebuchadnezzar was still at Riblah, he told Zedekiah exactly what he had to expect. The troops of Babylon were already over-running the province ; and the only serious resistance they encountered, beside the capital's, was at Lachish and Azekah. Jeremiah evidently had free access to the king ; but his words, if we may trust Baruch's narrative, were few (xxxiv. 1–7). " The city will be taken and burned ; you will be removed to Babylon, where you will die, and," he adds, " be

[1] See also on chap. xxxvi. 3, p. 121.

L

accorded royal honours at your funeral." The tone
of the prophet was very different from that which
he had used against Jehoiakim; and towards the
unhappy king it showed a certain personal regard.
Jeremiah knew the weakness and fear which crippled
Zedekiah; and against these foes Zedekiah had none
of Jeremiah's psychological defences.

Still, such language, which was not for Zedekiah's
private ear alone, was not to be tolerated; and
Jeremiah was forthwith arrested and imprisoned
in a dungeon within the palace precincts, where
he would be unable to weaken the city's morale.
The time had now gone by when a *défaitiste* could
be allowed to remain at large. On the other hand,
while he was there, Zedekiah could still consult
him (xxi. 1–10). Accordingly, two of Zedekiah's
entourage, the one a second Pashhur (ill-omened
name) and the other a priest, were sent to bid
Jeremiah inquire the purpose of Jahveh. It might
be necessary for reasons of state to silence the prophet, but his word still had its prestige. There
was no comfort in the response that came. Pestilence within the walls, the entry of the Chaldeans,
the massacre of the survivors, was all that the
prophet could now foresee. But with this message
to the king was coupled another to the people as
a whole; a message for which his enemies were to
make him pay dearly: " You have but one chance
of safety; to desert to the enemy."

This sounds like cowardice and despair. Had
the old man's spirit been broken? That there
were desertions is clear from xxxviii. 19; but he
himself refused to desert; so did his friends
Gedaliah and others. What Jeremiah was con-

cerned with at this moment was to emphasise at any cost the city's fate. To catch sight of the Chaldean lines from the walls of the city was, for the prophet, to see the victorious soldiery at their work of sacking the houses and slaughtering the wretched citizens. " So certain is all this," he said in effect, " that you will only save your own lives if you leave Jerusalem at once and surrender to the forces outside the gates."

The imprisonment, as we can well imagine, continued. And it brings us to an incident which Jeremiah himself and not Baruch has given us, and which, though it seems of purely personal significance, throws a unicue light on Jeremiah's prophetic consciousness (chap. xxxii.). His own account is this : Jahveh announced to him that his near relative Hanameel was on his way to request the prophet to exercise his right, or fulfil his duty, as next of kin, in purchasing a plot of land on the family estate at Anathoth.[1] Hanameel actually came and made the request. Then Jeremiah " recognised," as he says, " that it was a message of Jahveh," and, with the professional help

---

[1] To understand Hanameel's claim, it must be remembered that in Israel estates were regarded as owned by family groups, but within these groups individual members of the family had their own holdings. That it was usual to cling to these tenaciously is shown by the story of Naboth (1 Kings xxi.) ; but when the holder fell upon hard times, it might be necessary for him to raise money by selling his plot. To prevent permanent alienation, the next of kin was expected to come forward as purchaser. The next of kin had other duties besides. If the holder of a plot died without leaving an heir, the next of kin might be required to marry his widow, so that the succession might be preserved. Ruth iv. and Deuteronomy xxv. both describe procedure that was followed when the next of kin was unwilling for any reason to do this.

of Baruch, duly and formally carried out the transaction.[1]   But the whole proceeding seemed absurd.
The plot of land in question was actually at the
moment in the hands of the enemy.   Jeremiah
tells us that he represented this to Jahveh, and
that Jahveh replied that nothing was too hard for
him ;   that the city would be completely destroyed,
but that the fugitives would subsequently return
and settle down securely in the country, in an
enduring covenant with Jahveh, so that land would
in the future be bought and sold without let or
hindrance.

What lies behind this dialogue ?   The answer is
instructive.   Preoccupied as he was with the public
calamity, Jeremiah knew of the difficulties of his
family at Anathoth, which, being on the north
side of the city, would be peculiarly exposed to the
enemy.   Some of his family (possibly he was
thinking specially of Hanameel) would want to
raise money, if they could, on the land, as the land
itself would now be no good to them ;   and it would
be his duty, if appealed to, to purchase the plot
and make the payment.   It would not be strange,
we can imagine him thinking, if Hanameel were to
come to make the request.   And Hanameel came.
At once Jeremiah saw that there was more in all
this than a mere coincidence.   It was a warning
from Jahveh which must involve some deeper issue.
So the request was granted and the transaction
completed.   This Jeremiah felt to be imperative
—the command of Jahveh.   But no one could
overlook the futility of the whole purchase.   The

---

[1] The formalities appear to be rather more elaborate as described
in our present Hebrew text than in the Septuagint translation.

witnesses would be sure to point it out. "Here am I," the prophet might have said, "certain that the whole land is doomed, and buying a plot on the estate as if the enemy were beyond the horizon." Then came the further thought. "I have predicted ruin; but that is not the last word. If Jahveh has brought about this sale, as he manifestly has, by showing me that he sent Hanameel to me, the country will return to settled conditions. My old anticipations of a restoration and a new covenant are clearly confirmed; if I buy this land now, we shall all be buying land in the future."[1]

So the matter might have been described; but Jeremiah, as usual, interprets all his thought in terms of a conversation with Jahveh; everything that passes in his mind is either a word of his to Jahveh, or a word of Jahveh to him. And here, as always, the first or more natural thought, with a touch of perplexity, hesitation or compunction in it, is identified as his own; the second, resting on what we know to be his more abiding convictions, is the divine reply. What is here of special interest is his recognition that what is to us quite a natural anticipation becomes to him, when it is verified, a word from Jahveh; and that, as such, it turns an ordinary business transation into a vehicle for the re-affirmation of his profoundest beliefs.

Unhappily, for his future peace in the city, this message was not published. What was known and remembered was that he talked as if he were a friend of Babylon. Zedekiah might be impressed. Baruch

[1] Chap. xxxii. contains a prayer of Jeremiah (after the completion of the deed) and a long address by Jahveh on the past wickedness of Jerusalem, which are probably expansions of much briefer originals.

and a few others might be sure of his inspiration. But a prophet's " thus hath Jahveh said " was clearly not held by the public to be a self-evident truth, whether the prophet's other behaviour was normal or not ; and that Jahveh had really spoken by Jeremiah, most people did not suppose for an instant.

Meanwhile, conditions in the capital were growing more and more difficult. The blockade was felt more severely, and the long-expected help from Egypt did not come. A desperate expedient was now proposed, namely, that the Hebrew slaves in the city should be set free (xxxiv. 8–20). These unfortunate persons were mostly debtors, who had sold themselves and their families to their creditors as a sort of bankrupt's composition. The thing is constantly done in India to-day. And in Israel, as in many other communities, it was recognised by established custom and law. As labourers on their creditors' estates, these enslaved debtors would be useful enough, and their lot was often happier than that of the hired labourer whose wages, as we know, were not seldom withheld. Often they would be on quite friendly and even confidential terms with their owners.[1] Cooped up in the city, they were in a different position. Food and lodging and some sort of occupation had to be found for them, and all this was increasingly hard to come by. They might be more useful, and certainly less burdensome, to their owners, if they were set free. They could certainly be used for purposes of defence. Hence the proposal for their liberation. It is interesting to note that the

---

[1] A good instance of their friendly relations is seen in the story of Saul's journey with his father's slave (1 Sam. ix. 3 ff.).

matter was not made the subject of an order. Whatever the authority of the king and his ministers in these critical days, it was not absolute. There was indeed an ancient prescription that all Hebrew slaves should be emancipated after a period of six years, unless they chose to remain slaves for the rest of their lives.[1] But we do not know how far this was enforced. For most of the laws attributed to Moses, no " sanctions " were provided. Apart from the king and public opinion, there was in fact no one to enforce them, and neither of these authorities could always be relied on.[2] At this crisis, however, no appeal was made to the old custom. The liberation was to be unconditional, and it was to be a matter of general and formal agreement rather than of decree. The whole proceeding was democratic rather than bureaucratic or compulsory.

Shortly afterwards, news was brought that Hophra's forces were on the move. A wave of intense relief passed over the city, the more so as the Babylonian commanders were disturbed by the fact. They had no mind to be attacked in the rear. Hophra could be faced better in the more open country to the South than in the rocky and broken hills round Jerusalem. Accordingly the siege was raised, and the Babylonian troops left the neighbourhood of the city.[3] Life at once became more normal. Work outside the walls could be resumed. Cheap labour was needed, and the liberated slaves were brought back. This

---

[1] Exod. xxi. 2 ; cf. Deut. xv. 12.
[2] Jeremiah implies (xxxiv. 14) that the law was not obeyed.
[3] Chap. xxxvii. 5.

roused the anger of Jeremiah.[1] Doubtless he was asked what had become of his prediction, when the last of the Babylonian regiments was seen retreating across the hills. But he had his own way of looking at politics. Like the other prophets, he cared nothing for social or economic advantages. But a covenant—an agreement confirmed by an oath—was sacred. Its discharge was something owed not to man but to Jahveh. The sin was against Jahveh, and not merely against the unhappy slaves. The covenant itself, he felt, was noble. It went far beyond the venerable but neglected custom that dated from the first entrance into Palestine. Its infraction was an impiety. It would be punished as such. "You yourselves will be liberated," he continued in a tone of grim irony, "but only to a slavery of your own ; to the tyrants of sword, famine, and pestilence." Nebuchadnezzar's army would be brought back, and would accomplish the destruction so often predicted.

It is easy to understand Jeremiah's special indignation at this breach of contract. Profoundly sceptical as to the religious value of ritual, and persuaded that it formed no part of Jahveh's demands from Israel, he was more eager than any ordinary priest was likely to be for what he considered to be the real law of Moses, and of Jahveh —common honesty and consideration for the poor and helpless. This was the law whose neglect was hurrying the nation to its fate, and in this last act of high-handed cupidity, he saw only another and more flagrant proof of the hopeless corruption of

[1] Chap. xxxiv. 17 ff. Note that, from verse 7, Jeremiah has been set at liberty.

the nation. His countrymen, thinking of Hophra, might say, "Jeremiah is mistaken again." He, thinking of their deep-seated sin, was the more sure that every word he had spoken was from Jahveh.

The sorely-tried Zedekiah, whose personal fate was referred to by the prophet in every announcement of the city's destruction, sent another message to Jeremiah (xxxvii. 3–10); this time, a request for prayer. The reply was as stern as before. "Hophra's army will retreat. His diversion is only temporary. The Chaldeans will return. Even if you yourselves had defeated them, the wounded survivors of their army would rise up and burn the city."

But Jeremiah's days of freedom in Jerusalem were numbered. He took the opportunity of the absence of the Chaldean army to try and visit Anathoth, perhaps to look after the property for which he had lately become responsible. As he was leaving the city by the Northern gate, he was arrested by the guards posted there as a deserter. He protested, but in vain. Irijah, the captain of the watch, sent him to the officers in Jerusalem, and they, on their own responsibility, delighted to have him at last in their power, flogged him and confined him in an underground prison. This was a far more serious matter for the aged man than the guardroom in the palace, and it would perhaps have proved fatal, if another summons had not come from the distracted Zedekiah. Zedekiah was more afraid of his officials than was Jeremiah, and the prisoner had to be brought to him without their knowledge. Jeremiah's message was only what it had been (xxxvii. 17–21) : " You will be captured by Nebuchadnezzar." He added a request that the conditions of his own imprisonment might be lightened. The king agreed, and he was transferred to the palace guard-room once more. Zedekiah did not dare to set him at liberty.

But even then he was not to be left in peace (xxxviii. 1–13). In the guard-room he could still address the bystanders ; and to the military leaders, the effect of these addresses could only be to break the public courage. By this time, too, the Chaldeans had probably returned ; conditions were worse than ever, and the need of a desperate resistance was imperative. Four of the officers therefore went to the king and demanded some more drastic treatment for the prisoner. Zedekiah, with a gesture of helplessness, bade them do what they liked with him. From very early times Jerusalem has been undermined with tanks or cisterns. In the absence of wells or aqueducts, this was the only way of securing even a moderately valuable water-supply. Into one of these, underneath the guard-room in the palace court, Jeremiah was let down. The water had leaked out—" broken cisterns " were no new thing in the city—and he was left in the filthy sediment at the bottom. Here he might miserably have perished. In the famine to which the whole city was reduced, his captors would hardly have troubled to ration him. A Soudanese eunuch in the royal household, however, took pity on him and appealed to the king to be allowed to save him. Zedekiah was not prepared to have Jeremiah's death on his conscience. He wanted to be able to consult him still ; and

perhaps, if the worst came to the worst, Jeremiah
might prove a friend at court with Nebuchadnezzar.
That his attitude hinted at some understanding
with the Babylonian authorities could hardly be
denied. The necessary order was given. Jeremiah
was drawn up from his abominable prison, and
placed once more in the guard-room. His release
may well have seemed to him an act of mercy as
miraculous as was Peter's escape from Herod's
dungeon.

The situation grew still more desperate, and
Zedekiah determined on another interview with
the prophet. Summoning him to one of the
chambers in the temple set apart for the royal use,
he asked him the old question ; was there any chance
of escape (xxxviii. 14 *ff.*) ? Jeremiah hesitated.
He had but one answer, as Zedekiah well knew.
Was the king's question a plot ? Would it come
to the knowledge of his personal enemies ? If so,
would not the result now be not imprisonment
but death ? The long confinement could not
shake Jeremiah's conviction, but it was beginning
to have its effect. Pain and solitude have broken
younger men than Jeremiah was now. Zedekiah,
however, swore that the prisoner's life should be
safe. " Then," came the reply, " Jahveh's message
is—surrender, and you will save yourself, your
household, and the city; hold out, and you will
bring ruin upon all."

Another Jehoiakim might have rejected the idea
with scorn or despair. And Zedekiah too rejected
it, but for a different reason. " What if the
Chaldeans should hand me over to the Jewish
deserters in their army ? " " It is not their

insults you need fear," replied Jeremiah. "Jahveh has shown me a vision of another kind : the women of your own harem in the hands of the Chaldean officers, and taunting you, as deceived by your own favourites, and then deserted " (xxxviii. 22).

It was a pathetic dialogue ; the aged Jeremiah, bowed down by his sufferings, and dreading, as a weak and tortured man might do, further violence ; Zedekiah still in the prime of life, but torn in two by his fears of the rival parties among his own subjects. Like another ruler in Jerusalem, he was scared by the prisoner before him, and he tried to evade the force of his words, but in a different fashion from Pilate's. "Tell no one of our talk, if you wish to escape death," he said. "If the officers learn of this interview, you must pretend that you were petitioning against a severer imprisonment." Jeremiah must have seen through the rather pitiful subterfuge. It was for himself that Zedekiah was afraid. Yet both men were in considerable danger. In that hour of panic, any act of violence was possible. Jeremiah agreed, and subsequently gave to the officers the account which Zedekiah had suggested (xxxviii. 24–28).

The incident has been related by Baruch in a good deal of detail. As his manner is, he makes no comments. But the impression left on the reader is unhappy. Surely Jeremiah might have done more than present Zedekiah with these two cruel alternatives. Was not some word of sympathy or encouragement possible ? Could he not have attempted to rouse the king to some sense of dignity or patriotism ? And how could he acquiesce in the deceit which the wretched Zedekiah suggested ?   To ask this, however, is to misunderstand both the nature of prophecy and the character of the man.   Jeremiah said nothing more to the king because he had no further message.   Wearied and baffled as he was by months of conflict, he could still pity the king, but his mind had nothing else within it than the one conviction of the city's capture ; and he could speak and think of nothing else. Whether he was paralysed by the horrors of fire and sword that rose before his eyes, or felt that events must now run their course, the emotion and the pleading of earlier years came to an end during the siege ; and in the absence of any fresh dominating thought or prophetic inspiration, with that fear of death which is often strongest in moments of weakness and exhaustion, he followed the timid suggestion as pointing to the line of least resistance for them both.

The end now came quickly (xxxix.).   The defenders were at the last gasp.   The walls were breached and the enemy broke into the city. Zedekiah and the garrison made a frantic attempt to escape to the South across the hills of Judah ; but they were captured and brought to the dreaded Nebuchadnezzar at Riblah.[1] A punishment as brutal as Jeremiah had ever hinted was inflicted on the king. After seeing his sons killed, he was blinded and then carried off to captivity. The palace and the temple were burnt ; the fortifications were razed. The larger part of the survivors, along with the deserters, whom Zedekiah had so

[1] The fact that his headquarters were here on the Orontes shows that Nebuchadnezzar felt it more important now to be near Phœnicia than Egypt.

much dreaded, were taken to Babylon.[1] Enough
of the poorer classes, however, were left behind to
carry on the cultivation of the land. Nebuchadnezzar, anxious to the last to govern the province
through native rulers, placed at the head of affairs
Jeremiah's friend, Gedaliah, the leading repre-
sentative of the men of 621. That he ventured to
do so is proof of his own belief in the loyalty of the
pro-Babylonian party in Jerusalem; and, as we shall
find later, he even left in the province some members
of the royal family. Ebed-melech, who had rescued
the prophet from the cistern, was saved, as Jeremiah
had foretold (xxxix. 15–18).

Jeremiah himself was dragged off in chains with
the other exiles;[2] but when the caravan had tra-
velled a few miles, it reached Ramah. Did Jeremiah

---

[1] *Cf.* p. 129. How large was this deportation? Was the
country actually left virtually uninhabited? In the last chapter
of Jeremiah (an independent historical notice, not found in the
parallel narrative in Kings) we are told of three deportations by
Nebuchadnezzar, the first in 598, 3023 Jews; the second in
587, 832 inhabitants of Jerusalem; and the third in 582, 745
Jews—4600 in all. The narrative in Kings gives two numbers for
the first deportation—8000 and 10,000. The first two numbers
given in Jeremiah amount to nearly 4000. If we multiply
this total by four, to include the women and children, and
assume that the whole population of Jerusalem before the deportations was roughly equal to that of the same district at the end of
the last century, we should conclude that about a quarter of the
population of the city had been removed in 586. How far the
country was depopulated the narrative in 2 Kings (xxv. 12) will
perhaps suggest.

[2] The brief historical appendix added later on to the book
(xxxix. 11–14) relates that when the city was captured Jeremiah
was released from prison and handed over to Gedaliah; but the
account followed in the text (xl. 1 *ff.*) is probably from Baruch's
own memoirs, and is at once fuller and more likely to be correct.

remember when he saw Rachel's tomb there, the voice of weeping he had heard before (p. 82)? The Babylonian officer in command of the party discovered his presence there, and set him at liberty. "Your own God," he said, "has condemned Jerusalem ; you have made this plain, and are not likely to cause trouble. You may therefore accompany your countrymen to Babylon, or you may join Gedaliah at Mizpah." [1] This was a respectful tone to which Jeremiah had not been accustomed. He took the rations which were offered him, and departed to Mizpah to join Gedaliah. He had the satisfaction (if he desired it) of knowing that every one of his predictions had now at last come true. The land was desolate and stripped of the best part of its population ; and he was a homeless wanderer in it. Such was the reward of the prophet of Jahveh (xl. 1-6).

The prophet of the New Covenant was the spectator of a blow which might well have shattered the memory and the hope of any covenant. Nor did Jeremiah ever repeat his promise of twenty years before. But the belief that brought that prediction to the birth had never left him. And if he now utters it no more, it remains indelibly fixed in the heart of the true Israel of God.

[1] This sentence is implied by xl. 2 and 3, though not actually recorded.

IX

THE LAST STAGE OF
THE JOURNEY
586–? B.C.

xl., xli., xlii., xliii., xliv.[1]

THE path of the just, we are told, is like a light
which shineth more and more unto the perfect
day. But many just men have had to follow a
very different path. Jeremiah's life is like a series
of days beginning with an uncertain and threatening sunrise, and then clouding over into a gloom
which, though broken by shafts of sudden radiance,
brings on a troubled and starless night. If it were
not for his own conspicuous courage, and the
consciousness that in his deepest thoughts was the
movement and utterance of God, he would surely
have been of all men most miserable.

The first weeks after the fall of the city and the
prophet's return from Ramah to Mizpah were
such a dawn as this. For the moment, as he
looked round him in his new home, there were
welcome grounds for hope. The officer in command of the community, Gedaliah, was the one
public man on whose friendship and support he
could rely. Gedaliah too, as his premature fate
was to show, was a man of generous disposition

---

[1] From Baruch's memoirs.

and chivalrous instincts ; and his choice of Mizpah
as his headquarters showed a masculine grasp of
the situation. The modern Neby Samwil (the
reader will remember the importance of this
position in the campaigns of General Allenby in
the autumn and winter of 1917), it is about 300
feet higher than Jerusalem, and the middle point
of the central ridge. It commanded alike the old
territory of Ephraim (now destined to grow
relatively important again) and the descent to the
Shephelah and the coast.

Moreover, the complete destruction of the old
Davidic state removed every element against which
Jeremiah had protested for years. National independence was at an end ; and Gedaliah himself,
by tradition an opponent of the so-called " patriotic "
party, was not the man, nor was this the time, to
attempt the old policy of defiance to Babylon.
The temple had fallen ; the priests had gone.
No one could now hope to gain the favour of
Jahveh by the sacrifices which he abhorred. At
last the way seemed clear for the spiritual worship
for which Jeremiah had pleaded all his life. Were
not the chartered survivors at Mizpah the men
on whose hearts the new covenant might be
written ?

The country, too, was not entirely helpless.
Gedaliah had some more or less disciplined native
troops with him, as well as a force of Chaldeans ;
some of the ladies of the royal household had been
left behind with him ; this would hardly have
been done if the country had been reduced to a
desert. And although the land had suffered from
months of foreign military occupation, plenty of

M

food was still available ; the preceding harvest had been good, and the fugitives who had hidden themselves in the surrounding territories began to return. The prospects of Gedaliah were modest but bright, and his wise and kindly measures make us wonder whether Ezekiel was thinking of him when some fifteen years later he drew his picture of the " prince " in the restored city.[1] And though the temple and the altar were destroyed, the site was still there, and worship of some kind was carried on even yet amidst the ruins (Jer. xl. 7–12, xli. 5).

As far as Baruch's memoirs go, Jeremiah took no part in public affairs under the new regime. The respite from violence and persecution must have been welcome to the old man, and several writers have suggested that it was in these halcyon days that his thoughts, like those of Ezekiel, turned with a new hope and expectation to the future. They would accordingly place in this period the composition of that part of chaps. xxx., xxxi., which has been called the Book of Consolation. But even if the " book " is homogeneous, the reasons against dating it here are very strong. (See App. I., pp. 211 ff.) And these quiet days were very soon to end. Gedaliah had more enemies than he allowed himself to suspect. The neighbouring states, which, like Judah, had been permitted to survive Nebuchadnezzar's invasion, could not be expected to welcome the growth of a rival under the fostering care of a Baby-lonian favourite. And among the Hebrews left in Palestine, the fanatical hatred of everything

[1] Ezek. xlvi. Ezekiel's prince, it is worth noting, was not a member of the Davidic house.

Babylonian was not dead. A certain Ishmael, himself connected with the royal family, had been left behind, or had escaped from Judah, and commenced an intrigue with the King of Ammon. Probably, like the *émigrés* of 1789 in France or of 1917 in Russia, he was thinking of a restoration; and the high-spirited Gedaliah, refusing to take warning, was assassinated after two months of authority. This calamity was almost like another Megiddo. It was to bring chaos into the new order. Ishmael, like many another royalist re-volutionary in history, had little but violence to fall back on. He was at once attacked by Gedaliah's officers, Johanan and others, and driven back across the border to Ammon, where we hear no more of him (xl. 13–16, xli. 1–11).

But in spite of this success, Johanan and his friends were panic-stricken. They expected that Nebuchadnezzar would do nothing less than visit the murder of Gedaliah on them. Their only safety, they imagined, lay in flight into Egypt, where a number of Jews, they knew, were already settled. Perhaps, too, their own consciences were not entirely free from guilt. Still, they felt some hesitation. To remove into Egypt would be a further act of disobedience to Nebuchadnezzar, and if they were stopped before reaching the Egyptian frontier, their fate would be all the worse. They would have incriminated themselves. Hence, they determined to consult Jeremiah. The prophet had hitherto been silent. No warning had come from him to beware of Ishmael. Did he think that his life's task was now fulfilled ? Had the mental reaction after the fall of the city been

too much for him ?   Or had he so concentrated on
that event that he had no mind to probe the future ?
Now, however, Johanan and the others appeal to
him as an oracle, as David might have consulted
the priests, or Nebuchadnezzar the sacred arrows
of divination (xlii. 2 *ff*.).   " Ask Jahveh to tell us
what we are to do ; to go to Egypt or to stay
here."   Jeremiah consented, simply binding them
to accept the decision, whatever it might be.
Then he waited for ten days.   We are reminded
of another interval, when he was dealing with
Hananiah, before the authentic message arrived.
When at length he knew what to say, he summoned
Johanan and the others to his presence.   His
address is given with specially full detail by Baruch,
as we see later.   Baruch had on this occasion a
special personal interest.   And yet what Jeremiah
said might have been said, one thinks, without a
moment's hesitation.   It was at least involved in
all his previous addresses, and indeed in his whole
attitude.   " Jahveh's word is that you are not to
think of removing to Egypt.   Your only safety
lies here, under the protection of Nebuchadnezzar.
Jahveh will see that you are prosperous and safe.
But if you decide on the journey to Egypt, you
will simply be giving yourselves up to sword, famine
and pestilence."

This response suggests three interesting re-
flections.   First, Jeremiah's point of view is the
same as during the siege.   Subjection to Babylon
is the divinely appointed policy, and it will be
crowned with prosperity.   What is new, though
by no means contradictory, is the fierce threat in
case the response is neglected.   Second, there is

no moral guidance. The only ground for condemning the plan for flight is the desire to find peace and safety in Egypt (verse 14). Jeremiah's hearers might well have asked why he objected. In his previous addresses Jeremiah did not trouble to give his reasons for the necessity for making peace with Babylon, nor for his strong preference of Babylon to Egypt. Nor can we now say what those reasons were. All we know is that although the connexion between Judah and Egypt had on the whole been close and fairly friendly throughout the period of the monarchy, the greater prophets, as far as our information goes, had always been definitely opposed to it; that Nebuchadnezzar had higher conceptions of government than any Egyptian king; and that, for centuries after the fall of Jerusalem, the real strength of Judaism seemed to lie in the Jewish community in Babylon rather than elsewhere. Thirdly, Jeremiah's prophecy was not fulfilled. Johanan's party disobeyed Jeremiah's advice and went to Egypt; but the fugitives did not all perish miserably. Jeremiah might indeed have expected that they would. He might have argued, consciously or unconsciously, that Nebuchadnezzar would soon make himself as powerful in Egypt as Ashurbanipal had been nearly a century before. But in any case, he was wrong, and the prediction, whose preservation does credit to the fidelity of Baruch, must have left people asking yet again, "Can he really foretell the future"?

The answer is that Jeremiah did not pretend, save in a very limited way, to foretell the future. He did not even profess to do anything at all save

announce the message which had been delivered
to him. Now he was aged and wearied and perhaps
a little numbed in his thought. He could not for
a time be sure. As he might have said, Jahveh
did not make up his mind for him. When the
change came, however, we can see the old convictions reasserting themselves. What he had been
sure of before he was sure of still. Flight into
Egypt was wrong; and therefore, he added, with
a narrow and bitter concentration of thought, it
would be followed by condign punishment.

The tone of this address shows that Jeremiah
suspected what the attitude of his hearers would
be. And in this he was not mistaken. They
refused to connect it with Jahveh at all. They
angrily put it down to the influence of Baruch
(xliii. 1-7). "Baruch is a pro-Babylonian, and
wants to hand over good patriots to Nebuchadnezzar." This seems a wild accusation; but
Baruch was probably both socially and politically
a more influential person than his revered friend,
and in those ten days the two men might well
have talked over both the past and the future.
The fact remains that the fugitives, when, neglect-
ing Jeremiah's advice, they went down to Egypt,
did not find ruin there. Whatever the moral
dangers of life in Egypt might be (and these we
shall learn subsequently) the world in general and
the Christian Church have certainly gained as much
as they have suffered, in the long run, from Jewish
Hellenism in Egypt. We may deplore Tahpanhes;
we must be grateful for Alexandria.

Johanan and his associates started forthwith,
taking a large part of Gedaliah's company with

them, including the royal ladies. Egypt had for some time offered a warm welcome to foreigners— to Jews among the rest. Recent discoveries have given us a number of Aramean inscriptions, pre- sumably of Jews, on rock-tombs east of Tel-el- Amarna, in the reign of Psamtik I., a contemporary of Manasseh. We also have very full details of the life of a Jewish military colony at Aswan, in Upper Egypt, close to the second cataract. This colony was certainly in existence in the time of Psamtik II., shortly before the fall of Jerusalem ; and there are grounds for thinking that its members had migrated to Egypt before 621. These Jews, at least from the time of Cambyses, possessed a temple of Jahveh, which they did not at all regard as schismatic or contrary to any law known to them ; but by the side of Jahveh they worshipped at least four other deities, known as Anath, Bethel, Herem, and Asham. The first two names are clearly connected with localities in Palestine, one of them being, curiously enough, the home of Jeremiah. We cannot of course conclude that other Jews settled in Egypt maintained the same worship. But it is at least very probable that the Jews in Egypt kept to what may be called the pre- deuteronomic religion of Palestine, and that it is this form of religion which the fugitives of 586 would find when they came in contact, in Egypt, with the Jews who were there before them. If Jeremiah knew this, as he naturally would, we have another reason for his dread of any removal to Egypt.

It was no new thing for him to be disbelieved. But disbelief, though now and then it might make him hesitate, could never shake his conviction. Once in Egypt, he expanded his previous prediction. The Jews would perish, because Nebuchadnezzar, now turned again into their relentless foe, would come and make himself master of Egypt. With a return to that fiery certainty of earlier days which forced itself into the outlet of symbolical action, the old man dragged together some large stones, and buried them in the ground before the royal Residency in Tahpanhes, and then announced that on that very spot Nebuchadnezzar would set up his throne as a conqueror, and burn the Egyptian temples, adding a characteristic and very homely image which we may be grateful to Baruch for preserving (xliii. 8–13). Again history is compelled to shake her head. It is true that later on the Persians at one time seemed to have Egypt at their mercy. But Cambyses' attempt to insult the Egyptian religion was followed by very dangerous consequences. Alexander conquered Egypt; but his successors, the Ptolemies, were careful to respect the creeds and cults of their subjects. The power that destroyed the Egyptian temples was first Christianity and then Islam.

Meanwhile, the Jewish community was spreading. It had reached Memphis, the capital of Lower Egypt, and pressed southwards towards Thebes. No doubt it linked itself with existing Jewish settlements, though Baruch is silent on this point; and everywhere there appeared the old idolatry which had been temporarily suppressed in Palestine in 621. It roused the prophet to a long and vigorous protest (xliv.). We cannot gather from his words any details as to the precise cults which he had in mind, save that some of them were dedicated to the " queen of heaven." We are led at once to think of the worship of the " host of heaven " under Manasseh ; and the women who were carrying out the cult defended themselves by the naïve argument, " when we offered sacrifices to her before, we were well off ; when we dropped them, we suffered for our neglect." The women speak in the first person plural, as if the change had come in their own time ; this probably should not be pressed ; but their memory might easily go back for forty years.[1] The " queen " is probably Astarte or Ishtar, the Assyrian Venus, a deity whose character contained traits as diverse as that of the Hindu Kali. Jeremiah speaks as if her worship were inconsistent with that of Jahveh ; but this would not be necessarily so to her worshippers. Later on, as we have seen, the Jews at Aswan felt no such inconsistency. By a Protestant observer, the worship of the Virgin by a South European Catholic would doubtless be called idolatry ; the Italian peasant might reply that the offerings to the Virgin were the only things he knew of that would guarantee him good luck ; and that he was still a good Christian. Paganism changes its language, but rarely its nature, when it changes its ground or its country. The Anath of Aswan was almost certainly regarded as a consort of Jahveh, and could she not be called the " queen of heaven " ? Jeremiah was perfectly right. The

---

[1] We should notice also that their cult, as is generally held, has affinities with Assyrian worship ; it is not Egyptian. The influence of Egyptian religion seems to have been throughout most of the period of the monarchy strictly limited.

reformation of Deuteronomy had been only skin-deep after all. When the royal power which was behind it came to an end, the mass of the people forgot it.[1] They believed in ritual all the while, and in a ritual which was happier when it was hospitable than when it was forced to be exclusive.

Jeremiah, speaking once more in the name of Jahveh, recalls the protests of the earlier prophets, unheeded, and therefore resulting in the disaster fresh in the memories of all. " Why will you bring ruin on yourselves ?   Have you learnt nothing from the past ? " he asks. " Sword and famine and pestilence will fall on you. You will be execrated by all, and none of your race will be left to return to Jerusalem." The group to which he was speaking, especially the women, laughed at him. " You call this the message of Jahveh," they said, " but we care nothing for it.[2] We have resolved " (and the women appealed to their husbands as they added this) " to win back our old comforts in this way." Jeremiah does not dispute their facts ; he neither pleads with them, nor appeals to the converting power of Jahveh. But

[1] It is not altogether beside the mark to recall another religious reformation—that which was brought about by Akhenaten, the " heretic king " of Egypt, in the fourteenth century. He attempted to establish a real monotheism in his country ; but it disappeared for ever at his death. The fact that the ideas of Deuteronomy did not die out, although they fell into popular neglect, shows that they corresponded to the convictions of others in the nation beside a few " fanatical " prophets. But it may well be that they needed the alien soil of exile to preserve them, and that if they had remained in Palestine, they would have been choked.

[2] These words appear to mean that they did not recognise the message as coming from Jahveh, not that they refused to recognise Jahveh as their god.

he sees one thing now quite clearly. This outburst
of heathenism is the reason why it was laid upon
him that Jahveh was against the removal to Egypt.
And the result, he went on to say, would be that
the worship of Jahveh would become extinct in
Egypt, as indeed, to Jeremiah, it had already become.
In time this would be known as Jahveh's purpose.
And Hophra, he added, would be given up to his
enemies and suffer the fate of Zedekiah.

Such is the last recorded episode in the life of
Jeremiah ; an unavailing protest to a group of
superstitious women in a foreign land, and a
prediction which was not fulfilled. Hophra was
indeed given up " to them that sought his life "
(xliv. 30), if we may trust Herodotus ; that is, he
fell into the hands of the Egyptian party which
had deposed him. Jeremiah may have been aware
of the course which Egyptian politics even now
were taking. But no one who knew the history
of the Jews in Egypt would apply to it the expressions used by Jeremiah.

Of the rest, we know nothing. As with Paul,
the tale ends before it is done. Why did the
faithful Baruch finish when he did ? No one can
tell, any more than we can tell the reason for
Luke's strange silence at the close of the Acts.
Was Baruch sent by Jeremiah to Babylon, to find
a more reverent audience for his message there ?
Or did he try to tell the story to the end, and in
vain ? [1] Was Jeremiah's unfaltering fidelity to
his thankless task crowned in the end by the glory
of martyrdom ? We have the tradition of Isaiah's

[1] Readers of Virgil will remember Dædalus' fruitless attempt
to depict the fate of Icarus (*Æn.* vi. 32 *f.*).

martyrdom : as to Jeremiah, tradition is silent. Or perhaps there is an echo of some such fate overtaking him in the fourth of the Servant Songs, in Isa. liii.,—the passage which a recent writer, Sellin, would refer to another great servant of God whose end was unknown, no less a person than Moses.

The later Jews told another story of Jeremiah (2 Macc. chap. ii.), that at the fall of the city he took " the tabernacle and the ark and the altar of incense and carried them to the mount where Moses was buried and there he hid them to be reserved till the time that God should gather his people together." This Jeremiah would never have done, even if it had been physically possible. Yet there is a profound and mystical suggestiveness in the legend. On the surface, it would apply better to Ezekiel ; for Ezekiel carried away with him from Jerusalem all the priestly traditions in their purest forms ; when once the city fell, he set himself to the task of describing the restoration ; and " after God had gathered them together," Ezekiel taught, the temple and the altar were to shine forth in a new glory. But Jeremiah brought away with him something more momentous than the memories and hopes that centred round the shrine, a knowledge of God that sprang from the deepest and most secret movements of the heart, that could find room alike for the sternest and most unbending convictions, and for pleading, expostulation, faith, prayer, and an intimacy with the unseen that was as daring as it was pathetic.

And all this was manifested in a life which felt nervousness and self-distrust moulded into inflexible resolution, and the timid desire for pleasant human companionship transformed into the ardour of the saint who could fling himself upon God and rest there unmoved. Here, we might well say, is the ark and altar of the real faith of Israel; and we listen here to the authentic note of the deepest piety of the Old Testament. If we do not understand this, even Jesus must be something of a riddle to us. Has the time come when God has brought forth the treasure to His reassembled people, or is the secret hidden from us still ?

When the fortunes of Rome were at their darkest after the crushing defeat of the legions by Hannibal at Cannæ, the consul Varro, the one general who escaped from the slaughter, was received at the gates of the city by the Senators and thanked " because he had not despaired of the Republic." Jeremiah has been called the weeping prophet, and his message has been understood as one of sheer despair. The little collection of poems called Lamentations has been attributed to him, and his work has been thought of as one long lament. But no one who turns from a careful study of Jeremiah to Lamentations could credit him with its authorship. The poems suggest bewilderment, and almost stupefaction. Jeremiah was not bewildered. The disaster did not surprise him. He had expected it long before it came. He knew why it had come. And because he knew its reason, he could rise above its misery. He could meet it, not with despair, but with hope. It was not given to him, but to Ezekiel, to reconstruct the foundations of the Jewish Church. His life ended, as it began, with fruitless appeal and unsparing denunciation. But if his lyre had only one string remaining, that string was unbroken. He denounced because, after all, it was worth while to denounce. If his pleadings were of no avail at the moment, they were bound to bear fruit later on. His was not the easy optimism which believed that somehow when things were at their worst they must improve. His certainty that clouds would break rested on his conviction that their gathering and massing were inevitable. For his hope rested on God ; but a God who would not destroy injustice and callousness and hypocrisy could not be God at all. On the other hand, the very completeness of the destruction showed that the one thing God cared for was justice and peace on earth, and confident loving obedience in His people's hearts. And in the end what God cared for, He must bring about. Such is not the hope born of the cheerful beauty of a May morning. It is rather the hope that rises dim and austere in midwinter. But it is this hope which is the true yoke-fellow of faith and love, and for which a single star gives light enough to see God.

"If it be that thou didst show thy light, and yet seest not that any are saved thereby, nevertheless stand thou firm, and doubt not the virtue of the heavenly light. Believe that if they have not been saved now, they will be saved hereafter ; and if they should never be saved, then their sons will be saved ; for thy light will not die even when thou art dead. The just man passeth away, but his light remaineth ; and it is after the saviour's death that men are mostly saved." These words of Dostoievsky, true of many of the " humiliated and insulted " of the world, are truer of none than of Jeremiah. He showed his light, sometimes clear and gentle; more often stormy and livid. He could see none who were saved thereby. Yet he believed in the salvation to come. Through long periods the belief seems to have left him. But there is no more touching picture of a returning prodigal than in chap. xxx.; no nobler description of the new covenant engraved on the heart than in chap. xxxi. And if he himself saw the light but seldom, its quick flash smites across the mind's horizon more revealingly than the sunshine of a cloudless day.

Born for the cheerful friendships of the village, amidst the sights and sounds of the countryside, he was plunged into the fierce ebb and flow of a nation's life at the full crisis of its affairs; and he suffered all the woes he was forced to call down on others. He was bruised for their iniquities; the chastisement of their peace was laid upon him. But if Christ, who mediated salvation for all, and tasted death for every man, became the captain and completer of our faith, and the type and pattern of all good life, and yet needed that His sufferings should be fulfilled by the agony of His human servants, surely we may say that by the sufferings of that faithful servant of the Lord, as by many another of stern set brow and passionate wistful heart, salvation came the more surely to men. " In the sight of the unwise they seemed to die; their departure is taken for misery, and their going down from us to be utter destruction. But they are in peace. For though they be punished in the sight of men, yet is their hope full of immortality " (Wisd. iii.).

X

JEREMIAH AND GOD

We have now brought our study of Jeremiah's life to an end. We have watched the ebb and flow of his convictions and his emotions. Psychologically, we have had to deal with a complex problem, of the combination of passionate instability with a single and definite interpretation of history and life which never really changed. It would not be difficult to use all the modern technicalities of repressions, complexes, and defence mechanisms in describing such a life; to suggest that the eager and rather shy desire for simple human companionship, curbed and thwarted, issued in a stern refusal to have anything to do with normal family life; that quick susceptibility to the opinions of others became the rugged defiance of the man who had come to think of himself as a boulder or a walled city; and by way of compensation for the tendency to brood and hesitate, and to wonder whether others, with their experience and numbers, may not after all be right, we might point to the belief in constant illumination by the authentic voice and indubitable inspiration of God Himself.

The type is not wholly unfamiliar, though it has seldom been exhibited so clearly marked as in Jeremiah. To many it will seem unattractive; to his contemporaries, unskilled in the methods of

184

psychological analysis, it would be almost un-intelligible. But let the career be surveyed from the outside, and let the critic begin to appreciate the strength of the assaults against which the defences are set up, or the unmistakable value and sublimity of the convictions which are attributed to a wisdom more than mortal, or, again, the appealing tenderness of heart that survives every effort to transform it into a harsh and resentful isolation ; and then, like Zedekiah, we turn to him almost in spite of ourselves.

Sympathy makes every study of character interesting ; and Jeremiah soon arouses the sympathy of the thoughtful reader. But there is a question suggested by all that has gone before which will for many readers be of deeper interest still. What can we learn from Jeremiah about God ? Our concern is not really with Jeremiah, or any other hero of the past. Their lives have been lived ; the world has moved on ; we have to do with the present. If they speak to us, it is just in so far as their words were " not for an age, but for all time." Every great work of literature or art survives because it has in it something of the eternal. This is true of the writings of the Bible ; and the reason for the special place of the Bible in the literature of the world lies in the fact that so many of its readers, in every age, have found themselves brought into the presence of the eternal with a directness and assurance otherwise unknown.

But this is not all. We may study Jeremiah's convictions about God, and find them of abiding and increasing suggestiveness. But the question of chief importance is, What *is* God like ? What

N

does He expect of us, and what may we expect of Him? Even for those who are inclined, more or less explicitly, to deny either that God exists or that He takes the trouble to enter their universe, these questions are the last to be definitely set aside. And when we are dealing with such a man as Jeremiah, who waged the whole warfare of his life in bringing what he held to be the message of God to other people, we should do scant justice to our study of him if we went no further than this. "What I am," he would be the first to say, "or what I think, matters nothing. What God is matters everything."

But can we rely on the distinction? Can Jeremiah, or anyone else, show us "what God is like"? To put the truth bluntly, God can only be known through man's conceptions about Him. He writes no message on the rock or the sky. Even when men think they hear a divine word from outside, no one else hears it; which is as much as to say that the voice is not outside at all, but within. Our own thoughts are shaped and moulded by the thoughts of others; we edge or polish them with other thoughts of our own. Even those who learnt of God directly, as they would say, from Jesus, heard words that came from human lips, and from a human mind behind them; and when Jesus Himself heard words from heaven, they only heard what they took to be a rumble of thunder, or perhaps an angel. If we would learn about God from others, we must learn what they thought about God.

Happily there is no one from whose conception of God we cannot learn something; for no two of us are quite alike, and no one has a world of thought entirely closed to another's. But the thoughts of such a man as Jeremiah are of special worth. He gave himself up to the companionship of what he felt to be God, as few have done before or since ; he devoted every moment of his life, literally, to communion with God. Until we too have done that, and with his intensity of purpose, we cannot despise the results of such concentration. He has been conducting investigations, that is, which few of us are prepared to conduct for ourselves. As we have no results of our own, we must examine his. Even if we think of Jesus, and ask if we have not the final truth in Him, we must either conclude that we can safely neglect every one else who ever lived, or we must sometimes turn, even from Jesus, to one who bore, not for three years only, but forty, the contradiction of sinners, and who with strong groans and tears learnt by the things that he suffered.

Jeremiah, however, was no theologian. He did not set out to discover what God was. He did not examine His attributes or work out any creed as to His functions. Indeed, he can hardly be said to have thought *about* God at all. He gives us no glowing pictures of God's power over nature, like Amos or the second Isaiah. Even when he is perplexed, and allows us far more clearly than most prophets to see his perplexity, he speaks to God instead of arguing about Him. When he describes the actions of God, or His ways with men, it is in the manner of one who sees, and who has not to consider or calculate what he says. Nor does he ever strive after consistency. He is assured that God is consistent ; that His character and acts are " straightforward " or righteous ; but he never tries to explain a seeming contradiction.

Again, he is no mystic. The mystic took little interest in outside affairs. It was his own progress to God on which he concentrated his attention. In spite of certain noteworthy exceptions, like Catharine of Siena, and, to a less extent, St Teresa, one might read the great body of mystical writings and never guess what was the state of the world in which any particular author was living. How different the prophets. They rarely trouble about their own relation to God. They may indeed suffer bitterness of spirit, dejection, and even despair. But it is the sin of their countrymen which fills them with horror, and the destiny of their country which inspires them with their wild and soaring hopes. The mystics do not preach. The prophets do little else.

What strikes us first, in reading Jeremiah, is that to him Jahveh is a distinct person ; one who talks to him and with him, who commands, instructs, asks questions and answers them, and has his own plans and designs as he has his own hopes and fears.[1] He is powerful, but not omnipotent, for he may be defied. He is stern, but not relentless, for sometimes he longs to pardon. And Jeremiah talks with him as a trusted and indulged servant might talk with a revered but yet companionable monarch. Moreover, Jahveh has a special interest in the

[1] It will be observed that where the text of this chapter refers to God as the Christian thinks of Him, capital letters are used for the personal pronouns, and small letters, as elsewhere, when reference is made to Jahveh as conceived of by Jeremiah.

nation of Israel. Not that his standard of judgment for other nations depends on their conduct towards Israel. Favouritism of this kind is not unknown in the Bible, and it is common in other forms of religious thought; it is absent from Jeremiah. But while the wickedness of other nations rouses his anger, the wickedness of Israel affects him like the disobedience of a child or the infidelity of a wife. Jahveh, too, as it were, has " given hostages to fortune."

Moreover, Jahveh does not always choose to gain his ends by the simple exercise of his own power. He prefers to use a human being as his tool or his agent.[1] What he might have done himself, the prophet is to do. And, as if he were unable to make himself heard by the people, he commits his message to the prophet, and he even seems uncertain at times whether it will be effective or not. For the most part, however, he is content that it should be delivered, even though he is sure it will not be heeded.

The tool, Jeremiah learns, is to be used both to tear down and to build up. But, unlike Ezekiel, whose constructive work began five years after his call, Jeremiah has to give almost all his strength to the former of his tasks. Jahveh speaks as if he were forced to command this; and though the word falls most often on deaf ears, Jeremiah himself feels its awful power, like a flame or like a hammer smashing stones and rocks, and, if the prophet should attempt to resist, twisting and thrusting

---

[1] Compare Ezek. xxxvii., where the " exceeding great army," lying on the open field like so many dried-up bones, is to be raised to life by Ezekiel's prophesying " to the four winds."

him back to his work, and setting his whole body on fire. No wonder Jeremiah complained at such usage; and, worse still, when, like an overworked tool, he was battered and scarred by the hardness of the material on which he was used, he was neither spared nor considered, but, as it would appear, used all the more. Sometimes the prophet pleads for a mercy to the people which Jahveh will not grant; sometimes he on his part cries out for vengeance on a group of enemies or an individual opponent, and the prayer is granted.

Again, Jahveh cannot build up unless there is repentance. But for repentance Jahveh looks in vain. He cannot command it. He can only implore and threaten. Both methods turn out to be useless. Yet some means of restoration there must be. After all, Israel belongs to Jahveh, and Jahveh cannot let the nation utterly perish. He does not say to Jeremiah, as he says to Ezekiel, " I am not doing this out of love for Israel, but for my own name's sake." He pities; he remembers the affection of the past; he hears the lament of his people in their misery. He does not say, as with Second Isaiah, that they had suffered twice as much as their sin had deserved; but he gives them the repentant heart; and he restores them to the happiness of a simple country life. He is no war-lord, who will lead them to glorious victories over their national oppressors or hurl the armies of the enemy into the vast caves of Sheol. Nor will he turn the over-crowded insanitary little citadel of Jerusalem into a fair and symmetrical city that might be the envy of Damascus or Babylon. He devotes his gifts to the country-side, with its quiet prosperous agricultural work, its cheerful home-life, and its simple joys of wedding feast and village dance.

Jahveh's character is thus, at least on the surface, a strange medley of contradictions. The prophet's master, we might almost say, needs analysis like the prophet himself. He is stern and fierce, yet relenting and tender. At one moment, his message to the prophet exhausts language in describing the miseries to come on the unhappy and stiff-necked nation, without a word of either compunction or pity ; at another he would give his people chance after chance to repent. Now he is like the God of the medieval Christian, whose terrible hell waits for the unrepentant among His creatures as surely as His purgatory and His heaven are prepared for the penitent and forgiven. Now he is like the God of the modern universalist ; he will have all men, or at least all Israelites, to find salvation. He condemns and he pardons ; he destroys and he saves.

We cannot but be reminded of the familiar words, uttered with a very different meaning, " thou thoughtest that I was altogether such an one as thyself." The outlook of Jahveh, as Jeremiah describes it, is strangely like that of Jeremiah himself. For Jeremiah too moves between the two opposite poles of hope and fear, sympathy and harshness. He resents angrily the intrigues of his kinsmen at Anathoth. He repeats Jahveh's fiercest words without a hint of sorrow or regret. Yet at other times he will intercede for the very race he condemns, and he longs that his eyes might be a fountain of tears to be able to express in floods of weeping the sorrow that drains his heart. What is all this but to see him projecting himself into his God, and giving his own message under the august disguise of the word of Jahveh?

The theory is plausible, but it has three difficulties to meet. First, these oscillations between hope and fear, or between the mood that cries "perish" and the mood that cries "repent," are not peculiar to Jeremiah. They occur in most of the prophets. They are specially striking in Hosea, whose sky was as lurid as Jeremiah's; and they are a part of that wide-spread outlook on the world known as Deuteronomic. If they belonged to Jeremiah, he shared them with all the serious thinkers that had gone before hin. We should therefore have to admit that by "Jahveh" we meant the quintessence of prophetic thought, and not simply the mind of Jeremiah.

But, more than this, there are times, as we have seen, when Jeremiah is conscious of being rebuked and corrected by Jahveh. He would spare; Jahveh would condemn. He would utter all that comes into his mind; Jahveh would have him separate the valuable from the worthless. It may be, as we suggest elsewhere, that "Jahveh" corresponds to the inmost convictions of the prophet; he is certainly not the projection of the prophet's whole mind.

The third difference is more important. Jeremiah sees in Jahveh what the other prophets have seen; but he sees something else; or rather he sees it with a clearness that is his own. Jahveh tries the heart; that is, he looks not at a man's actions merely, but at his thought and purpose and will. It is not simply that he sets no store by ritual and is wearied by sacrifice and feasting or days of public humiliation. It is not even that he demands acts and abstinence of another kind—prompt payment of wages and debts, due regard to the complaints of the poorer classes (as we should call them) and reverence for the family virtues. Jeremiah does not indeed say that all this, by itself, is worthless; nor, like Paul, that the most heroic self-sacrifice is useless without love; but he does assert the principle that in the eyes of Jahveh it is the motive that makes the difference.

This, some will object, is the simplest and most elementary axiom of all sound ethics. It may be; but even to-day there are heated discussions which would vanish if it were once recognised. And the point is not that we all agree, or think that we agree, with Jeremiah to-day, but that he did not find the truth to his hand as we to-day find it to ours. Nor is this quite the bald ethical statement that some would suppose. To say that it is the motive which matters to Jahveh is more than to say that Jahveh is not deceived by appearances, whether he has to deal with the vulgarity of a Pecksniff or the half-conscious self-worship of a Willoughby Patterne. Jahveh who tries the heart is the Jahveh who talks to Jeremiah without ceremony, as man to man, listening to all his rash and hot-tempered complaints, and answering him, not out of the whirlwind but in the natural tones of everyday intercourse. He does not choose temple-court or storm-ridden sky for his theophany, but the simple aspects of ordinary life; he might not even disdain the homely " kettle whispering its faint undersong."

Others have known that Jahveh looks on the heart of a man, or have learnt his purpose from a basket of ripe fruit, or a plumb-line hanging off from a slanting wall. To do justice to Jeremiah we must observe that Jahveh judges the thoughts because it is in the world of the thoughts that he moves. He desires no sumptuous worship, he points to no arresting glories ; he plans no dramatic return for his people ; he builds them no shining city. Appearance is valueless to Jahveh in conduct because it is valueless to him in everything else. Nothing matters but the simple personal affections, and when his prophet is inspired to describe the future that his grace will ensure, it is always the future of a simple community with " household motions light and free," and, if we may quote Wordsworth yet again (not forgetting how sur-prised the poet would be at the comparison), " true to the kindred points of heaven and home." [1]

Undoubtedly we have here the fundamental preference of Jeremiah. A score of passages have shown us his love for the homespun happinesses and pieties of the village. Others have shared this. What they have not shared is his conviction that to appraise men God tries their thoughts by this test. To find such teaching again, we must look at the incarnate Word of God lying in an improvised cradle outside a noisy khan, or listen

---

[1] It is characteristic of the simplicity of Jeremiah's conception of his intercourse with Jahveh that he never once mentions Jahveh's " spirit " or " breath " : here he is in specially strong contrast to Ezekiel.

to the sentence according to which a man's eternal destiny is decided by his neighbourly gifts of clothing or his visits to jails.

Jeremiah's conception of God, then, is complex enough. In part we can trace it to his predecessors, though, like every great artist, he touches nothing that he does not make his own. In part, we must trace it to himself, observing how, to some extent at least, he puts his own thoughts into the lips of Jahveh, and how, besides this, he discovers to us a distinct and individual view of the world, which is a part of himself, and of which Jahveh is the centre. But, when all this is appreciated, we have still to ask what Jeremiah's conception of God, striking and individual as it is, has to do with God as He is, and therefore with us. Did the prophet invent it, or unconsciously develop it, or receive it from some external source ? Or did he receive it, as he thought he received it, from God ? If so, how do we account for its limitations ? If not, what was its source ?

To attempt to answer this question, we must look at Jeremiah's messages from a slightly different angle. We have been considering the prophet's general conception of God ; but he himself claimed to be an actual reporter of Jahveh's words. The phrase " thus hath Jahveh spoken " is common to all the prophets ; and although in some instances it is perhaps an addition to the text (especially where it is absent in the LXX), it is too frequent, and its use too individual, to be discounted. But is there anything in the claim ? Did God give to the prophet the words which he repeats, or did He not ? If He did, we surely have a revelation

as to the character of God that is of the first importance ; if the phrase is to be understood in any
other way, and Jeremiah and the other prophets
were deluded or self-deceived, how can we take
them as serious religious teachers ?

The dilemma has not often been faced.   But
the fact that, like men and women in other ages,
they claimed to hear a divine voice surely raises a
problem for the theologian as well as for the
psychologist.   We can only approach it usefully by
considering the prophecies in some detail.

Let us take first Jeremiah's denunciations.   The
speaker is uniformly represented as Jahveh ; but
the words are clearly mixed, as we have seen, with
human feelings.   The actual predictions are sometimes categorical, sometimes conditional.   Beyond
the mention of Babylon, and a general statement
as to the length of the Exile, the only details given
are the imminent deaths of Pashhur and Hananiah.
Speaking generally, it must be said that no new
truth is announced, and nothing is predicted for
which, to a student of previous prophecy, and a
competent observer of current events, either a
special revelation or a gift of clairvoyance would
be necessary.

The promises, mostly in chapters xxx. and
xxxi.,[1] are unrelated to the rest of the book, and
are as much " in the air " as the Servant Songs of
the Exile.   We are left asking, as in the case of
the threats, whether, for such predictions as these,
a revelation was needed at all, or whether their
very vagueness does not suggest the faith of a

[1] Chap. xxxiii. contains at most some reminiscences of
Jeremiah.

man who, for all his habitual anticipations of gloom and horror, or it may be because of them, could not put aside the conviction that at last, far off, all that there had been of good in the nation's past should live again in some more beautiful form.

What then are we to make of Jeremiah's experience at his call? Did he think that Jahveh laid a hand on his mouth, and that he subsequently began a conversation with him, and said, "The tree wakes, and I wake too"? Or was it the truth that Jeremiah was holding a conversation with himself? "What is that? An early-waker; and Jahveh must be waking over his people; I am sure of it; and his waking must be for their punishment." A little later: "There is a kettle, looking away towards the North; from the North come invading armies; and they will come upon us." This is all the more natural if, as we have before suggested, the youth has already felt like another Hamlet that the times are out of joint, and (as perhaps the other Hamlet had felt even before he saw his father's ghost) that the person to put them right would be himself. It may be that when the vision came, the certainty of a mission came also, as the fulfilment not of a conviction or even of a wish, but of a dreadful but unlikely possibility, which had been previously repressed. We seem in any case to be dealing (if the psychologist will allow us to say so) with two layers of consciousness, of which the second and deeper one is identified by Jeremiah with Jahveh himself. No doubt the communications from this lower layer came with such clearness and force that he could say that he heard them. Augustine said the same thing when he described his conversion in the garden at Milan. Whether, if we had questioned Jeremiah on the spot, he would have said that he *felt* his mouth being touched is another matter.

In the next place, we have noticed in Jeremiah's ministry a number of what may be called acted texts for sermons. These are not always, one would think, even particularly effective texts. In two instances, the burying of the girdle in the Wady Farah until it was spoiled, and the hiding of the stones in the brickwork at Tahpanhes, we can only suspect that the prophet is finding relief, by some striking and laborious piece of self-expression, from pent-up and fierce emotions. It is noteworthy that when, in chap. li., Seraiah, Baruch's brother, is told to sink in the Euphrates the roll of denunciation against Babylon, the action is not attributed to any command of Jahveh, but is given us on Jeremiah's own authority.

The visit to the potter (chap. xviii.), the breaking of the bottle (chap. xix.), the incident of the yokes and the envoys of the confederate states (chap. xxviii.), and the interview with the Rechabites (chap. xxxv.), all seem to imply a sudden intuition, doubtless partially obscure ; and when it is carried out, a further piece of insight. The actual situation which the prophet is led to construct creates by way of response the utterance of a definite conviction. When this conviction is ready for utterance, Jeremiah hears, and announces, the word of Jahveh. In the episodes with Hananiah (xxviii.) and Johanan (xliii.), Jeremiah has to wait for the certainty to come. In the negotiation with Hanameel (xxxii.), the surmise becomes later on the certainty.

Still more instructive are Jeremiah's conversations with Jahveh. The colloquies would be quite as intelligible if, remembering Tennyson's well-known poem, we were to head them, *The Two Voices*; " a still small voice spake unto me. . . . then to the still small voice I said "; the only difference being that the attitude which Tennyson ascribes more particularly to himself is the attitude which Jeremiah connects with Jahveh. The one voice, which Jeremiah calls his own, expresses an attitude of which he is acutely conscious; it is mobile, and liable to sudden emotional changes; misgivings, regrets, complaints, and rushes of sympathy and indignation. It is met by the utterances of a steadfast and immovable conviction which shames or awes him into acquiescence and acceptance. The mind, we might say, is here replying to itself, either by way of rebuke or the fulfilment of some underlying desire. The important point is that when the thought arises which carries conviction with it, even though the conviction is accepted with reluctance and strife, it is identified with Jahveh. We might formulate the equation, " The voice that brings acceptance and assurance is the voice of Jahveh."

And yet Jeremiah recognised that the confident " Thus hath Jahveh said " was not in itself sufficient to attest the message. The false prophets could make the claim as well as he. Some external test was at times necessary in order to establish the fact that Jahveh was the source of the prediction.

To prophesy deliverance was something in itself to be suspected. But the genuine message of Jahveh was more than a mere message of destruction. The prophecies of blessing which both Jeremiah and Ezekiel have given us, go far beyond the simple predictions of escape which they both quote from their opponents. At bottom, Jeremiah knew that he was right and his opponents wrong, because he knew that he was interpreting history ethically, and that it could be interpreted in no other way. It may be that the other prophets were sure that their messages were correct. But if we asked them how they knew, they would have answered, " Anything else would be too horrible." Jeremiah's answer would be, in our language, " Anything else would show Jahveh's existence to be a delusion." And this is the last word of faith.

But are the predictions true ? Clearly, the predictions of the fall of the city were fulfilled. To foretell that event needed no abnormal revelation. But what of the prophecies of final restoration ? It cannot be said that they have been fulfilled, or are ever likely to be fulfilled, with any approach to exactness. Yet, as they stand, they are the consequences of the prophet's most assured beliefs. Jahveh had bound himself to Israel; therefore Israel could not possibly perish in the end. But Israel had sinned desperately ; therefore Israel could not be saved or restored as she was. It followed that Israel must be changed ; and then all would be well. For the most part, the second of these two promises occupied Jeremiah's attention. But it was this very fact which drove him to his conclusion. And even if, in uttering these convictions, he used expressions which could not have been used by one who saw the future as clearly as the past, his words may yet be said to lead to the fundamental truths of the Gospel.

Most readers will feel that if Jeremiah leads up to the Gospel, we can be confident about the truth, and perhaps about the origin, of his words. But if we revert to the prophecies already examined, with this in mind, we shall find them leading us right away from the Gospel. If we are to regard Jahveh as in any sense responsible for the form of the predictions of destruction, or as the interlocutor of Jeremiah in the dialogues already discussed, we can hardly avoid a surrender to Marcion and his view of the God of the Old Testament, as a God who was radically opposed to the God of the New. Whoever he is, this Jahveh cannot be the God and Father of our Lord Jesus Christ. We may justify the spirit of the words as noble and elevated, if we think of them as coming from Jeremiah ; but many of them are wholly foreign to all that Jesus has taught us to think of as divine. We may admit that the destruction was inevitable. Some would even admit that it came upon the nation as a punishment for its political coquetry, social greed, and religious laxity. But it involved terrible suffering for the innocent as well as for the guilty ; and if God Himself had seen fit to announce it, as Jesus announced the calamities that were to follow His death, would tones of anger and severity alone have been heard, and pity and even sorrow have been silent ? Even Hosea makes Jahveh hesitate when he has to give up Ephraim to ruin. But

o

with Jeremiah, there are many times when the only pity that we hear is from the lips of the prophet, not from Jahveh. Can we suppose that God would have left Jeremiah to wail, " Oh that my head were waters and my eyes a fountain of tears ! " while He Himself cried out, " Shall not my soul be avenged on such a nation as this ? "

To Jeremiah, then, his own deepest certainties are recognised as words of Jahveh. Whether we too are to regard them as such or not, we can see how, like independent powers, they deal with him. They rise before him in their awful sombreness. They terrify him. He shrinks from them. They pursue him. They master him. They force him to utter them. Then they fade away. Their forms are dimmed by his fears or his grief or loneliness. He argues with them. All that, to our minds, is most attractive and human in him rebels against them. But sooner or later, they compel him to give way. And, now mounting on the flames of his indignation, now half drowned by his tears, they find speech. They are indeed to him the message of Jahveh. And when a whole discourse is given as Jahveh's word, we can see how with the passages of deepest emphasis the impressive attribution to Jahveh is repeated.

Yet when all this is admitted, our earlier question returns on us. What have Jeremiah's conceptions of Jahveh's message to do with the actual word of God ? Is it not as difficult to argue from the one to the other as it is to argue from Jeremiah's conception of God to God's eternal character and will ?

The wisest theologian might well hesitate here.

Final or complete truth in Jeremiah's words he cannot accept. Yet, if there is no revelation as such in Jeremiah, can he be sure of it even in Jesus? There is a revelation; but we shall only find it if we are content to form our idea of revelation from such facts as we have studied in Jeremiah, and do not bring to Jeremiah a ready-made conception of our own. God does not speak to us *ab extra*. His messages come from within. He writes them, as Jeremiah would say, on the heart. They arise from the deepest level of the prophet's own mind. They are his thoughts. They could belong to no one else. And so far as he is the child of his time, of his race, or of his creed, so are they.

This, however, is only half the truth. If it were the whole, we should be pushing the doctrine of immanence into pure subjectivism. Yet to say that the truth is written on the heart is more than a metaphor. The prophet recognises the truth as distinct from his own thoughts. And the message, like the fire or the hammer or the hand of the writer, moulds, turns, bends, and finally satisfies the mind which receives it. This powerful current which wells up from inside the consciousness is in it yet not wholly of it. It flows in from the outside, as the ancients fabled the waves and seas of their own little world to flow in from the mighty stream of the encircling ocean.

But in truth we must get rid of these spatial terms. When we are thinking of God, we cannot think of space. "Where is God? Inside or outside us?" We might as well ask, where is thought, where is beauty, or even where is *a* thought ? However mysterious thought may be, we know that it is not in the brain, or anywhere else. Nor, to be precise, can we think of man, any more than of God, as being in space. His body is. But the body is not the man. To say that man is not in space does not mean that man is not in his body, and therefore outside it. It means that when we speak of men, or of God, we cannot use the term inside or outside at all. God is not less God because He cannot be thought of as acting on man like an external force. If we are to suggest a comparison, He acts on man as thought acts on thought, or as person acts on person.

Thus, thoughts may be said to rise in the mind ; voices are heard ; tasks are set. As the grammarian would say, we must use the passive voice ; we cannot be satisfied with the reflexive. It is not a case of hearing or seeing ourselves. Were the high influences which moulded the life and freed the energies of Joan of Arc any less real because the voices could have been heard as little by Charles the Dauphin as by La Hire, or because she gave them the imaginary names of Michael and Catharine ? The fact is that she was influenced and affected, and that something did for her what she could never have done for herself. So with Jeremiah, the prophet whom, of all his goodly fellowship, we know best. The shrinking youth was taken, set apart, thrust forth, tempered, developed, transformed. The high influence had laid its hand on him.

To all this, the psychologist has his answer. It is the answer which we ourselves may seem to have suggested. The high influence is just that part of Jeremiah's own nature, it will be said, which he did not recognise as his own, but which was none the less the foundation of all his conscious experience and activity. But this is a mistake. There is nothing in common between the buried "phobes" and suppressed wishes, unsuspected by their possessor until some wise physician "analyses" him, and the powerful convictions to which Jeremiah gave utterance; convictions which are neither neuroses nor desires, but stern and dreaded pronouncements of the future or interpretations of the present. They are as different from the neurotic's feeling that he must touch all the posts he passes in the street as the deep-seated devotion of the patriot or the saint is different from the restless disquietudes of the ailing infant. They are commands; but when they are obeyed, something else is perceived—the strong support, the firm guidance, the assured protection, which Jeremiah came to know better than he knew himself.

That is how Jeremiah, as he would have said, knew God. The voice spoke; and when Jeremiah responded, the voice answered again. The hand pointed, and when Jeremiah touched it trembling, the hand grasped his own like a vice. He leaned upon the command; he knew it to be a living spirit. Jeremiah knew God as some one distinct from himself; not simply because He informed Jeremiah of things of which he was himself previously ignorant, or because He showed him things he could never have seen by himself; but because He acted towards him as a personal influence and power. God's intercourse with Jeremiah was not merely a matter of fresh elements in his intellectual apprehension ; it changed his whole being.

Thus, when we are dealing with what we have called Jeremiah's deeper layers of consciousness, we are dealing with very much more than a kind of thought which any of us might have without being aware of it. Just as little are we dealing with a secondary personality or an abnormal break-up of the conscious ego. It is true, indeed (and we need not shrink from admitting it), that we may detect a far-away resemblance to the pathological " co-consciousness," as it is now called, suggested by the cases studied by Dr Morton Prince and others, where the patients have felt themselves aware of other beings who are really themselves in another state or stage of consciousness. But the resemblance is indeed far away ; for in those cases the two consciousnesses alternate ; A does not co-exist with B, even though A may be conscious of the existence of B, and B of A. Moreover, A and B, so far as they really are aware of one another, are rivals ; and seem even to struggle for the possession of the same body and the same friends.

We have only to mention this to see how entirely different is the " possession " of Jeremiah. He is not only aware of Jahveh ; he talks with Jahveh ; he is influenced by Jahveh ; and he draws from his intercourse with Jahveh a strength and assurance and firmness of character that, as we have seen, are foreign to anything we know of his own nature. Jahveh is to him the source and origin of his insight, his persistence, his comfort and his hope. And how else can we ourselves describe God in

His relation to our inner lives ? We have already affirmed that the terms " outside " and " inside " can have no applicability to the relations of God to the soul. God is neither " outside " nor " inside " our consciousness. He is within us ; and to say that what takes place within us cannot be from God is no argument, since what is from God could take place in no other way. The Christian knows that the voice of Christ also is heard, if it is heard at all, within the soul ; and when the cross is seen, it is seen, as Jeremiah saw his almond-tree or his cauldron, with the eye of the soul. God is not recognised by His invading the consciousness in some peculiar way from without ; indeed, such an invasion would be quite unthinkable. He is known by the new capacity, the poise, the effectiveness, the purity and strenuousness of soul, that results from His presence. Like the prophet of the old dispensation and the teacher of the new, He Himself is known by His " fruits." However we interpret or manipulate the facts of consciousness, the facts are that when a man throws himself on what he feels to be the power distinct from himself, waiting to support and guide and deliver, there manifests itself within him something that was not there before, that is at once the answer to his prayers, the fulfilment of his hopes and the very breath of a new life.

That is why the study of Jeremiah must always be of special value to any man who would understand his own religion. For Jeremiah reveals to us more clearly than anyone else a man who is conscious of God dominating, controlling and inspiring, even while the messages of God are obviously relative to his own time and outlook, and God Himself is obviously felt as distinct enough from Jeremiah to allow of personal intercourse between the two. It is also when we reach this point that we can answer the dilemma of our previous question; " either God did not speak to Jeremiah at all, or He did not speak the words of complete and absolute truth." The universe of thought in which He spoke to Jeremiah was that of Jeremiah, not that of Jesus, or of ourselves. God always speaks in the universe of thought of the men whom He approaches. And who are we that we should say that our universe alone is complete or real ? We shall no more think that God rebukes our feelings of sympathy or compassion because He bade Jeremiah denounce Judah, than we shall think that we ought to have treated Germans or Turks (or they us) as Saul was bidden to treat the Amalekites.

God did not come down to inspire the prophets as Virgil describes Apollo coming to inspire the Sybil. She resists the divine invasion to the utmost of her power ; but Apollo wears her out and moulds her to his will. Nor is Jeremiah to be distinguished from the " false prophets " by actually receiving a gift *ab extra* which they only pretended to have received. The secret of the prophets' greatness was not in what they came to possess, but in what they felt, and knew, and *were*. However they interpreted their experiences, God did not speak *to* them, treating them as mere passive listeners. He never speaks to any one in this way. He spoke in them, and through them. Some of them, indeed, were men to whom supernormal visions

and auditions were not unknown. Ezekiel certainly
seems to have experienced trances of the most
varied description. But these were only the
accompaniments of their activity. It is doubtful
whether, for Jeremiah, we need assume them at
all. What was essential was that there came
moments when the prophets were absolutely certain
—were carried across, so to speak, to the other side
of doubt. It is not strange that such an intellectual
experience should have brought with it an emotional
exaltation that bore down before it all opposition
both from without and within.

We apply to the prophetic words the only test
that can be applied—the test of Jeremiah himself ;
the test of the event. Not that we ask of them,
did the predictions come true ? Veridical prediction is no test of divine inspiration. We ask
whether, after making all due allowance, as we
must, for the temperament, the training, and the
outlook of the prophet, the words ring true. And
if they have proved themselves the words, and
the begetters of yet greater words, which have
been for centuries " a balm in sorrow and a stay
in strife," who shall say that the spirit of God
is not in them ? For we recognise the voice of
God in the assurance which grips the speaker as
in a vice, and then approves itself in the experience
and conscience of men. Truth, unlike truths,
cannot be written down in a book. It enters a
man's heart, grows into his thoughts, wells up as
from some unsuspected depths in his consciousness.
And if as it finds utterance in speech we can hear
the tones of the prophet's human voice, the prophet
knows that there is something more than human

in it, something that is of an abiding significance and that comes from the Eternal. And he is right.

We could not hear the deeper tones in the voice of Jeremiah if we had not heard the music that breathed in Galilee or that rolled from beneath the darkness of Calvary. But the richness of that music will not be fully understood till we have listened to the notes which, on the lips of the prophets, herald its triumphant yet poignant rise and fall. The one chord that is left to Jeremiah's music knows as little of the eager expectation of a day when the morning stars sing together as it knows of the varied and delightful harmonies of the gospel; but it has been touched by the finger of God—the God who causes light to shine out of the midst of the darkness, and who chooses the very moment of weakness and defeat for the birth of a new confidence and an unconquerable hope, and of the faith that overcomes the world. And when all discords are resolved in " the great C major of this life," the despised prophet of Anathoth will have his due place with all who

" Live with Him and sing in endless morn of light."

APPENDIX I

CHAPTERS XXX AND XXXI

THESE chapters, and especially the brief section on the New Covenant towards the end of chap. xxxi., have been more hotly discussed than any other part of the book. The whole prophecy of the return of the Northern tribes has been suspected because it seems to be so different from most of Jeremiah's predictions and from his general outlook, and also on account of the language of the chapters, which, it has been argued, is not only similar to that of some later prophets, especially the second Isaiah, but dependent on it. We do not propose to go into the arguments in detail here ; we have already urged (Chap. IV.) that the outlook of these chapters is by no means impossible to Jeremiah, while the argument from language is very far from proving dependence on the prophet of the Exile.

If, however, we allow that the two chapters, and especially the section on the New Covenant, belong to Jeremiah, to what part of his life are they to be attributed ? Several of those who have attempted to answer the question have turned to the brief interval in 586 when Judah, like Ephraim, had fallen, and when the prophet was enjoying a brief " Indian summer," under the kindly rule of Gedaliah, after the strain of the previous distracted twenty years. But it is very difficult to suppose that Jeremiah's spirit could have recovered so quickly from the stress and the misery of the siege ; and it is equally difficult to understand his tone to the survivors under Johanan (Chap. IX.) if these glowing predictions had immediately preceded. There is nothing to suggest that a return was then in his mind ;

still less when we read his uncompromising words to the Jews in Egypt.

Volz has found what he considers a suitable interval of calm in the earlier years of Zedekiah. But this supposition is really no easier. Chap. VIII. has shown that Jeremiah had no more faith in Zedekiah than in his predecessor, and that he was then as much oppressed by the thought of the coming ruin as before. Nor is there any more in the speeches uttered under Zedekiah than in the address in Egypt to suggest that Jeremiah had recently seen so alluring a vision. Cornill therefore attributes the prophecy to Jeremiah's earliest years, before 621, like the brief prediction of restoration in Chap. III. But although, even then, he felt that restoration must be Jahveh's purpose, he was chiefly impressed with the nation's sin and the certainty of some coming horror ; and although, as we agree, in speaking of the New Covenant, he was thinking of Sinai and not of the new code discovered in 621 in the temple, there is a distinct psychological difficulty in supposing that in his first period, with all his youthful and impetuous condemnation of the society around him, he could have arrived at so far-reaching a conviction as that expressed in chap. xxxi. 31 *ff*.

We seem therefore to be driven back on the view stated in Chaps. IV. and V. He had seen the promise of the reforming movement under Josiah, and he shared, at first, its hopes. These hopes, for him, with his deep sympathies for the Northern tribes now in exile, naturally take shape in the expectation of a return for Israel, which, with a mind free from the previous task of denunciation, he can elaborate with all the wealth of his poetic vision. But he is gradually filled with doubts as to the value of the reformation ; and as he sees its futility, his thoughts work back to the original covenant at Sinai. That Jahveh should allow that covenant to go by default he will not believe ; but since it finds no fulfilment in the reception of the new code, or indeed in the code itself, there must be a new covenant, written, unlike the Decalogue or Deuteronomy, on the heart, that is, in the thoughts and the

whole attitude of Israel. It is very probable that the
chapters in question have received later additions ; in
particular, the authenticity of the last two sections of
chap. xxxi., vv. 35–37 and 38–40, is more than doubtful.

But we may urge, as evidence of the genuineness of the
bulk of the two chapters, that the general conception of
the future is entirely characteristic of Jeremiah, and indeed
peculiar to him. There are no apocalyptic or even national
glories ; there is no king to achieve victory or reign in
righteousness ; the restored community simply comes
back to a land where it can till the soil and buy and sell in
peace and content. Similarly, the prophecy of the New
Covenant, though, if rightly understood, far more explicit
than anything else of its nature in the Old Testament, is
only what we should expect from chap. iv. 7 ; it has none
of the dramatic impressiveness of Ezek. xxxvi. or Isaiah liii.
All Jeremiah thinks of is the simple change of mind ; of
the passage from the outer rite, of circumcision, to its
inner equivalent, and from the outer ceremony, the reception of the two tables of stone, to their enshrinement in
the heart.

Finally, it may be asked why, if the chapters were written
in the reign of Josiah, they were not included in the book
read to Jehoiakim in 603 ? The introduction to the
chapters (xxx. 1–3) implies that the prophecy of return
was regarded as something distinct, and in Jeremiah's
mood in 603, desirous as he was of impressing the king
and the nation with the peril of the general situation, this
little treatise of consolation would hardly have seemed
relevant. It evidently maintained its separate existence ;
for when Jeremiah's remains were collected, it was not
included in the first part, among the prophecies (chaps.
i.–xxv.) but placed where we should hardly have expected
it, in the narrative section (xxvi.–xliv.), immediately after
the prediction of salvation in xxix. 22.

APPENDIX II

THE COMPOSITION OF THE BOOK OF JEREMIAH

THE book of Jeremiah as it appears in our Bibles has had a long and obscure history. Its nucleus is generally agreed to be the collection of prophecies which was made by Baruch under Jeremiah's direction after the destruction of the first collection or roll by Jehoiakim in 603 B.C. (see Chap. V.). Most writers hold that this collection included all that Jeremiah had written hitherto, or, at least, had chosen to preserve (xxxvi. 2); and this is what the text seems to imply. But if, as we have concluded, the prophecies of Israel's restoration and of the New Covenant found in chaps. xxx., xxxi., and the *journal intime* of colloquies with Jahveh were already in existence, it is none the less unlikely that they would have been included in the roll (see Appendix I). Whether the prophecies appeared in chronological order in the roll cannot be decided. The arrangement of the greater part of chaps. i.–vi., which must have appeared in the roll, seems chronological; but it is quite possible that Jeremiah was influenced, as we know that later editors were, by the wish to join together passages of a similar purport or character. The remaining sections of what must have been in the roll are scattered up and down the earlier half of our present book of Jeremiah.

Subsequently Jeremiah preserved, doubtless with the assistance of Baruch, a number of prophecies and one or two personal narratives. At the same time, or later, Baruch set down his account of a number of incidents in the prophet's life, chiefly relating to the later years in

Jerusalem and the period immediately after the city's fall, of which he was an eye-witness. These compositions were then put together by Baruch or some one else, the bulk of the addresses being placed first and the narratives afterwards. On the other hand there was so complete a disregard at times of chronology that the same event may be referred to in two different parts of the book (*e.g.*, chap. vii. and chap. xxvi.), and prophecies belonging to the reign of Zedekiah precede others which clearly belong to Jehoiakim. The colloquies are scattered about near the middle of the book, but not placed actually together. The whole was subsequently rounded off with a quite distinct account of the fall of Jerusalem (chap. lii.) which occurs in a similar though not identical form at the end of the canonical book of Kings (2 Kings xxiv. 18–xxv. 30).[1]

Still later, a collection of prophecies on foreign nations, by various authors, was formed. Some of these may be by Jeremiah ; the prophecy on Moab is very similar to that found in Obadiah ; the longest and most striking, on Babylon (l., li.), is certainly by a different author ; its attitude to Babylon is entirely different from that of Jeremiah ; and there is nothing in the other prophecies in this collection which, in the mind of the present writer, can be attributed with any confidence to Jeremiah. These prophecies have therefore not been referred to in the foregoing chapters. This collection was inserted at the close of the main book of Jeremiah, but before the historical appendix in chap. lii. ; and indeed the appendix may have been added after the prophecies on foreign nations had been incorporated with the previous collection. In the Greek translation, however, this section on the nations was placed in the body of the book, immediately after the references to prophecies against foreign nations in chap. xxv.

Even with this large addition the growth of the book did not come to an end. Several other passages of a clearly later date were embedded in the book, *e.g.*, chap. xvii.

---

[1] Observe how different chap. lii. is from the shorter but more vivid chap. xxxix.

19–27, along with a number of detached oracles or prophetic sentences, and remarks and comments by various readers which were perhaps originally entered in the margin (*e.g.*, v. 18 f., ix. 24 f., x. 11 (in Aramaic), xxxi. 26, xxxii. 17–23) and then found their way into the text. Later Jewish readers, with all their veneration for the great prophetic names, were not unnaturally anxious to secure all the fragments of prophecy on which they could lay their hands, and a large collection of prophecies attributed to some well-known name would easily gather to itself detached and floating fragments (*cf.* Isa. ii. 2–4 = Mic. iv. 1–3 ; Jer. xxvi. 18 quotes Mic. iii. 12), whether tradition-ally connected with some author's name or not. At least one section, not otherwise distinguishable from the rest of the writings of Jeremiah or Baruch, seems to have had an independent existence or to have been independ-ently edited, viz., chaps. xxvii.–xxix., where proper names combined with the Divine name (*e.g.*, Jeremiah, Hananiah) often appear in the shorter form (with -iah) instead of the longer form (-iahu) common in earlier Hebrew, where the form Nebuchadnezzar is found instead of the usual and more correct form with *r* (Nebuchadrezzar), and where differences between the Hebrew text and the LXX translation are specially numerous.

In the preceding chapters we have confined our attention to those sections of the book which we hold it possible to vindicate as belonging to Jeremiah or Baruch. But it must not be forgotten that if a section is taken away from the author whose name is borne by the book in which it occurs, it does not therefore lose its value, either for literature, for history, or for religion.

INDEX I

NAMES AND SUBJECTS

References to Jeremiah and Jahveh are found on practically every page.

A

Abiathar, 17, 84
Abraham, 1
Ahab, 1
Ahaz, 24, 26, 64
Ahijah, 42
Ahikam, 107, 115, 122
Akhenaten, 178
Alexander the Great, 176
Allenby, Gen., 169
Amaziah, 33
Ammon, 139, 171
Amon, 27 f., 63
Amos, 4, 6, 21, 30, 32 f., 43
Anath, 175, 177
Anathoth, 16 f., 27, 52, 84, 138, 155 ff., 161
Apries, *see* Hophra
Aristides, 2
Armenians, 80
Asa, 24
Asham, 175
Ashur-bani-pal, 25, 27, 31, 40
Ashur-uballit, 103
Assyria, 25, 27, 31, 40, 62 ff., 80, 99 f., 103
Aswan, 175, 177
Augustine, 59, 198

Aurelius, Marcus, 94
Azekah, 153

B

Baalim, 23, 42, 119
Babylon, 49, 147 ff., 168 ff.
Bach, 15
Baruch, 11, 114 f., 120, 123 f., 132, 151, 153, 173 f., 179
Bethel, 175
Bismarck, 116
Blake, 6

C

Cambyses, 176
Carchemish, 116, 146
Catherine of Siena, 188
Cheyne, T. K., 12, 117, 126
Cobbett, 6
Coniah, *see* Jehoiachin
Cornill, C. H., 212
Covenant, 74, 78, 160
Covenant, Book of, 71 ff., 159
Covenant, the New, 39, 88 ff., 167, 170, 183, 211 ff.
Cyaxares, 100, 103
Cyrus, 136

D

Dante, 3
David, 1, 17, 42
Decalogue, 9, 48, 88, 212
Delphi, 42
Deportations, 129 f., 166
Deuteronomy, 70 ff, 91, 104,
    108, 111, 122, 148, 155,
    178, 212
Dostoievsky, 182

E

Ebed-melech, 151, 162, 166
Edom, 104, 139
Egypt, 62 ff., 68, 100, 103,
    109, 123 f., 129, 146, 171
    ff.
Elam, 25
Eliakim, *see* Jehoiakim
Elijah, 6, 110
Ephod, 41
Ephraim, 80, 161, 169
Esar-haddon, 25
Exiles, Jewish, 133, 135 f.
Ezekiel, 2, 3, 4, 6, 10, 36, 44,
    53, 82, 90, 93, 117, 136,
    148, 170, 180 f., 189, 194

F

Farah, Wady, 138, 198
Fox, George, 7

G

Gedaliah, 154, 166 ff.
Gemariah, 122
Gillies, J. R., 13
Giotto, 15

H

Habakkuk, 94
Hamlet, 3
Hanameel, 115 ff.
Hananiah, 140 ff., 148, 198
Harran, 103
Henry VIII., 75
Herem, 175
Herodotus, 55, 59
Hezekiah, 66 ff., 175
Hilkiah, 18, 28, 68
Hinnom, Valley of, 117
Hölscher, F., 70
Hophra, 146, 159, 161, 179
Hosea, 22, 30 f., 43 f., 73, 77,
    93, 121, 192
Huldah, 69, 78
Hutchinson, Col., 30

I

Irijah, 151, 161
Isaiah, 6, 22, 29, 34, 43 f., 53,
    66
Ishmael, 171
Ishtar, 177

J

Jahvist and Elohist, 21
Jehoahaz, 106, 109
Jehoiachin, 126 ff., 141
Jehoiakim, 94, 104, 106 ff.,
    122 ff., 126
Jehoshaphat, 24
Jehu ben Hanani, 42
Jesus, 8, 11, 112, 164
Joan of Arc, 46, 204
Job, 95 f.

Johanan, 171 ff., 198, 211
John, Gospel of, 151
Jonathan, 151
Josiah, 27, 31, 63 ff., 109

K

Keats, 15
Kent, C. F., 12

L

Lachish, 153
Lamentations, Book of, 181
Law and Ritual, 72, 74
Luke, 114, 151, 179

M

Maccabees, II, 180
McFadyen, J. E., 12, 46
" Magor-missabib," 57, 120
Manasseh, 24 ff., 104, 177
Marcion, 201
Mattaniah, see Zedekiah, King
Medes, 25, 31, 55, 59, 100
Megiddo, 99, 105 f., 148
Memphis, 176
Micah, 22, 43, 113, 121
Micaiah, 42, 45
Milton, 3, 29
Mizpah, 167 f.
Moffatt, J., 12
Mohammad, 7
Moses, 6, 85
Mozart, 15

N

Nabi, see Prophet
Naboth, 155
Nabopolassar, 100, 103
Nahum, 101
Nathan, 42
Nebuchadnezzar, 100, 116,
    124, 132, 149, 171 ff.
Neby Samwil, 169
Necho, 105 f., 116, 124
Nietzsche, 45
Nineveh, 101 f.

O

Obadiah, 215

P

Pashhur, 119, 137, 142, 154,
    196
Paul, 1, 4, 11, 36, 85, 91 f.,
    98, 114, 179, 193
Peake, A. S., 12
Peter, 1, 163
Plato, 144
Pottery, 118
Priests, 64, 89
Prince, The, 170
Prince, Dr M., 206
Prophets, 6, 41 ff., 65, 102,
    134 f.
Psamtik I., 25, 27, 59, 104, 175
Psamtik II., 139, 146, 175
Ptolemies, 176

R

Rachel, 82, 166
Ramah, 82, 166, 168

Rechabites, 125 ff., 198
Reformation, English, 83
Reformation, Jewish, *see* Deuteronomy, Josiah
Riblah, 153, 165
Roads, 19
Ruskin, 4
Ruth, Book of, 155

S

Sabbath, 48
Samaria, 80
Samuel, 6, 38, 41
Saul, 158
Scott, Sir W., 30
Scythians, 25, 31, 55 f., 100
Scythian Songs, The, 56 ff.
Sellin, E., 180
Servant, The Suffering, 39, 110, 180
Shakespeare, 3, 15, 50, 197
Shaphan, 68, 107
Shelley, 57
Shemaiah, 137, 142
Shiloh, 117
Skinner, J., 12, 95
Slaves, 158 ff.
Smith, Sir G. A., 107
Socrates, 52
Solomon, 17, 111
Spirit, The Holy, 194
Steuernagel, C., 104
Streane, A. W., 12
Subartu, 103

T

Tahpanhes, 174, 176, 198
Tel-el-Amarna, 175
Temple, The, 23 f., 32, 54
Tennyson, 199
Teresa, St., 188
Thebes, 176
Thomson, W. R., 13
Thucydides, 125
Tyre, 25, 139

U

Uriah, 115

V

Varro, 181
Virgil, 179, 208
Volz, P., 81, 212

W

Welch, A. C., 12, 70, 105
Wisdom, Book of, 183
Wordsworth, 3, 15, 29, 44, 57 f., 194

Z

Zadok, 17 f.
Zedekiah ben Chenaanah, 38
Zedekiah, King, 94, 130 ff., 154 ff., 179, 212
Zephaniah (priest), 137
Zephaniah (prophet), 27, 53 ff., 59

INDEX II

PASSAGES IN JEREMIAH

	PAGE		PAGE
i.	32 ff.	xiii. 1–11	138
ii. 2–4	46	12–17	115
5–12	49	18–19	127
29–37	50	xiv. 1–16	57, 101
iii. 1–5	50	xv. 5–9	124
19–25	51	10–21	97
iv. 1–4	51	xvi. 1–9	93
5–8	56	xvii. 9, 10, 14–18	96
13–17	56	19–27	216
18–22	57	xviii. 1–12	118, 198
23–26	57	18–23	87, 92
27–31	58	xix. 1–15	119, 198
v. 1–14	52	xx. 1–6	119
18–19	216	7–12	96
20–31	52	14–18	95
vi. 1–5	58	xxi. 1–10	154
6–21	52	xxii. 1–5	109
22–26	56	10–12	109, 127
27–30	53	13–19	111
vii. 1–14	115, 215	24–27	127
21–28	115	28–30	127
viii. 4–13	86, 115	xxiii.	134
ix.	128	xxiv.	135
24, 25	216	xxv. 1–10	128
x. 11	216	xxvi.	112 ff., 215
19–25	102	xxvii.	139, 199
xi. 1–11	79, 87	xxviii.	140, 198
18–31	84	xxix. 1–23	136
xii. 1–4	84	24–32	137
7–13	124	xxx.	81 ff., 170, 196, 211 ff.

	PAGE			PAGE
xxxi. 1–25	. 81 ff., 170, 196, 211 ff.	xxxix. 11–14	.	166 n.
26	. . 216	15–18	.	. 166
31–34	. 89, 211 ff.	xl. 1–6	. .	. 167
xxxii.	. . 155	7–12	. .	. 170
17–23	. . 216	13–16	. .	. 171
xxxiii.	. . 196 n.	xli. 1–11	. .	. 171
xxxiv. 1–7	. . 153	xlii.	. .	172 ff.
8–20	. . 158	xliii. 1–7	. .	. 174
xxxv.	. . 125, 198	8–13	.	176, 198
xxxvi.	. . 120, 214	xliv.	. .	176 ff.
xxxvii. 3–10	. . 161	xlv.	. .	. 123
17–21	. . 162	xlviii.	. .	. 49
xxxviii.	. 163 ff.	l.	. .	49, 215
xxxix.	. 165, 215 n.	li.	. .	. 215
		lii.	. .	. 215

STUDENT CHRISTIAN MOVEMENT